The Golden Mulligan

AND THE STROKE

THAT CHANGED THE GAME

The Front Nine: Where Life and Lessons Meet

By
Cella Renee

Allecram Adventures Publishing

Copyright © 2025 by Marcella Cotton, writing as Cella Renee All rights reserved.

No part of this book, including the P.A.G.E Power Method framework, may be shared, copied, reproduced, or transmitted in any form without prior written permission of the publisher, except for brief quotations in reviews or critical articles.

This is a nonfiction work for informational purposes. The events are described to the best of the author's memory. Some details, and identifying characteristics may have been changed to protect the privacy of individuals. The author and publisher make no guarantees regarding the outcomes of applying strategies shared in this book. The reader assumes full responsibility for their choices and actions.

Published by Allecram Adventures Publishing (an imprint of Allecram Adventures LLC) Birmingham, AL, USA
www.allecramadventures.com

ISBN: 979-8-9933076-1-9

Library of Congress Control Number: 2025921309

Cover design by the author; photographs by L. Jones Photography & Designs

Interior design by the author

PRINTED IN THE UNITED STATES OF AMERICA

First Edition: 2025

DEDICATION

To my daughters, my greatest victories in life itself. I love you both more than words could ever describe. You are the reason I believe that the purest love can conquer fear and that hope can rise from the hardest places. You have shown me that resilience is not only about getting back up, but about standing tall—with love, with grace, and with purpose. You have taught me how to apologize when I've made mistakes, and how to grow from them. You have helped me become a better mother and a better adult, always striving to be the best person I can be. You are my perpetual why—the reason I persevere. Thank you for listening, correcting, and cheering me on!

This book is for you, and anyone ever told their story didn't matter. May you always remember that your voice carries power, your journey holds meaning, and your course is yours to chart. Step forward with courage, fully embrace every second chance, and share the story only you can tell—your point of view, your narrative, your experiences, your truth, your light.

ACKNOWLEDGMENTS

Above all, I thank the Lord for His grace, mercy, covering, protection, and the abundance of blessings that reach far beyond me.

To my family, thank you for walking with me through both the fairways and the rough. To my father, whose quiet strength and love for golf planted a seed of passion and purpose within me. To my mother and sister, whose struggles and resilience inspired my voice as an advocate for healing and hope. To my brother, whose encouragement, laughter, and understanding give me strength when I need it the most, and to my grandfather, whose legacy of unconditional love continues to guide me.

To my extended family, friends, sorority sisters, community, and prayer warriors—you have been my village. Your encouragement, wisdom, and presence helped sustain me when I didn't have the wherewithal to stand on my own. Thank you!

To my inner circle, thank you for sharing sacred spaces with me during my darkest moments, I love you deeply and cherish our bond more than words can express. You know who you are. Thank you for being steady rocks in my life, helping to form the foundation of this journey.

To the golf community that believed in me—beginning with my golf coach at 3BM Golf Studio in Birmingham, AL. Thank you for your support, patience, knowledge, and encouragement. You reminded me golf is not only about mechanics, but mindset and resilience. Thank you to those of you who helped sharpen my skills in a welcoming space—on and off the course. SisterGolf, Lady Links Golf Club, First Tee—Birmingham, and RTJ Golf Trail at Oxmoor Valley Driving Range—thank you.

Special Mention to Clearview Golf Club in Canton, Ohio, and the legendary Renee Powell—thank you for allowing me to learn more about the game on a historic golf course that continues to pave the way for generations of golfers. Your kindness reminded me that golf is more than a game—it's a community.

Huge thank you to all of the golf mentors, and confidants who generously shared your time, wisdom, encouragement, and drills with me. Your guidance shaped not only my swing, but my spirit!

To Roebuck Golf Course in Birmingham, AL, thank you to the entire staff for always welcoming me with open arms and warm smiles. You acted F.A.S.T. with genuine support, care, and concern when I needed it most. Your efforts played a big part in my recovery. For that, I will always be deeply grateful.

To Ronda Robinson, thank you for taking the time to write the foreword and lending your wisdom to these pages. Your encouragement gave me the courage to use my voice in more ways than one. I'm grateful for your belief in me as a client and beyond! You have helped open doors for me far greater than I ever imagined, and you bring the essence of sisterhood to life!

And finally, to the readers, thank you for walking this course with me. May these pages remind you that no matter what the setbacks, handicaps, or stroke of misfortune life gives you, you can play through with courage, strategy, and a heart anchored in purpose.

FOREWORD

The game of golf may seem like a simple and leisurely game. However, those who truly understand the sport know it's a masterclass in resilience. One bad shot can rattle your confidence and one moment of precision can restore your faith. Golf is a powerful metaphor for life. Cella Renee is not only my friend, sorority sister and client - she is so much more. She has read and donated countless books to children within our local community and in Africa, ensuring access to storytelling and learning. She has broken barriers, challenged stereotypes, and inspired me both professionally and personally. Her remarkable journey from a moment of crisis to a new perspective on life is simply amazing.

The game has changed for this tireless professional, devoted parent and dedicated athlete. Having a stroke did more than challenge Cella Renee physically; it turned her controlled, purposeful, and skillful life upside down. Some may assume the game would be over for a person who suffered a stroke then endured emergency brain surgery but for her it was a transformation.

Resilience is not about bouncing back to who you were, but about adapting to who you are now. throughout these pages Cella Renee is raw, honest and at times funny as she shares her life story. This book is a roadmap for finding inner strength. Her experience will motivate stroke survivors, their caregivers, and anyone who has faced adversity.

Cella Renee discovered that her purpose was no longer defined by a perfect swing or a flawless scorecard, but by the courage to play the game differently.

Ronda Robinson

CEO

Carmine Communications LLC

TABLE OF CONTENTS

Introduction 1

Prologue: The Golden Mulligan 3

The Front Nine - Chapter 1: Course Management—Presence Over Perfection 101 7

Chapter 2: Some Rescues Are Rough 13

Chapter 3: Greens, Cornbread, And A Dash Of Hot Sauce 22

Chapter 4: The Breaks 31

Chapter 5: Stats, Handicaps, And Hats 36

Chapter 6: Hazards, Hooks, And Healing 41

Chapter 7: Get A Grip (On Yourself) 47

In Remembrance 57

Chapter 8: Build Your Bag One Club At A Time 65

The Front Nine Finale - Chapter 9: The Trinity 70

Epilogue 77

Message From The Author 78

The Golden Mulligan Journal Companion With The P.A.G.E. Power Method.™ 79

Chapter 01: Course Management Presence Over Perfection 101 84

Chapter 02: Some Rescues Are Rough 88

Chapter 03: Greens, Cornbread, And A Dash Of Hot Sauce 92

Chapter 04: The Breaks 97

Chapter 05: Stats, Handicaps, And Hats 101

Chapter 06: Hazards, Hooks, And Healing 105

Chapter 07: Get A Grip (On Yourself) 109

In Remembrance 113

Chapter 08: Build Your Bag One Club At A Time 117

Chapter 09: The Trinity 121

Closing Reflection 127

A Heartfelt Thank You 128

About The Author 129

References 130

INTRODUCTION

A mulligan in golf is a rare gift. A chance to reset, to take another shot as if the last one never happened. It's a second chance. On the other hand, a one-stroke penalty is entirely different. It's a setback, a reminder that precision matters and that every swing carries weight. Also, hitting the ball out of bounds costs you both distance and momentum. In both cases, you must start over. Sometimes from scratch. Sometimes from a less-than-ideal position. Either way, the game moves forward.

These moments can be frustrating for many golfers. Every player wants a perfect round, every drive straight, every approach clean, every putt true. But perfection is a fantasy, and a real golfer understands that the game is as much about handling the bad shots as it is about celebrating the good ones. Some days, your swing feels effortless, the ball soaring exactly where you intended. Other days, nothing goes right, and you find yourself trudging through the rough, trying to figure each frustrating stroke out. Yep, that's golf for ya! A game of resilience. A game of patience. A game that demands humility and rewards persistence. And in many ways, it mirrors life itself.

GOLDEN MULLIGAN

When I fully embraced the mental game of golf, I realized it wasn't just about playing against an opponent or even mastering the course. For me, it was all about playing against myself. Against my doubts. Against my frustrations. Against the part of me that wanted to quit after a bad hole. Inevitably, my inner warrior would emerge, determined to prevail, not just in golf but in life. And the driving range—that's my sacred place. It became my proving ground, where every challenge, every misstep, and every victory reflected the larger battles I faced off the course. I discovered golf is more than a sport. It's a test of character, a lesson in perseverance, and a reminder that no matter how many bad shots you take, there's always another hole, swing, or chance. And that's my game. On the driving range, the course, and in life.

PROLOGUE
THE GOLDEN MULLIGAN

I *magine this: you're playing your favorite game. Any game—and losing. Your opponent is basking in victory, and the crowd's going wild. You begin your awkward walk of defeat.*

You reach out your hand for a polite shake, already rehearsing your "good game" face, when something tells you to check your pocket. Weird, right? But hey, you've got nothing to lose—except your pride, and to be honest, that pride lasted about an hour—then your score reminded you that you were in a different league…the losing one.

After reaching deep into your pocket, you pull out a crumpled, well-worn piece of paper. The ink slightly smudged—used, but unfamiliar. You've never seen it before, yet it feels as though it has passed through many hands before reaching yours, destined for this very moment. Your heart skips a beat and your right hand trembles with a little fear as you slowly unfold the note. Your opponent pauses mid-smirk to watch. Then you see it in bold letters:

"DO OVER."

GOLDEN MULLIGAN

Wait… what?

You blink. Your opponent blinks. The crowd blinks. For a second there, you think you're dreaming, but it's real.

Turns out, you forgot this game allows second chances. Not often and never when you expect it. But when they show up, do-overs change the whole game. No protests. No rulebook rewrites. Just grace, served up quietly on a golden platter.

Now, picture this: a game of golf. Follow me. A little different—fewer fans, more grass and dirt stains, and the only cheering is from squirrels. You and your opponent finish the round, and you announce, "Mulligan." It essentially means you get a do-over. But not the usual kind you use after a bad swing. This one is not only paid for—it's earned. Sacred. And the plot twist? It shows up at the end of the game.

Unheard of, right? I knew you'd say that but remember this isn't your typical game of golf. It is personal. It is spiritual. The rules don't feel like they are written in a rulebook—more like etched in your soul. You could feel it. Something shifted.

Somewhere back there, you dropped the ball—maybe literally, maybe not—and now you're being asked to go find it. The place where the ball dropped. Thinking back, you remember that you gave it everything. But you're older now, in your 50s, and suddenly golf—this game that once brought much fulfillment feels funny. Strange? Unknown? Or perhaps it is saturated in clarity like never before.

That's when the note in your hand starts to make sense.

PROLOGUE: THE GOLDEN MULLIGAN

In golf, a mulligan is a do-over—a swing without judgment. It doesn't ask for credentials. It doesn't care about any handicaps you may or may not have. It's not about what you deserve, whether you're teeing off from the ladies' tee or otherwise. It's all about what you're ready for. And this mulligan? This one's golden. Not only because you're in your 50s—it's royal. It represents mercy and grace given to you by the highest level— an authority no one could ever challenge—and win.

You take it—not with an egotistical attitude, but with quiet gratitude. You realize this second chance isn't just about fixing your shot. It's about rethinking your game and maybe helping someone else do the same. Because divine gifts aren't meant to be hoarded, they're meant to be shared. You turn to your opponent. But by now, they're not really your opponent anymore. Just someone who's been through the rough at some point, too. You offer your hand as a gesture to extend grace and announce who you are.

"My name is—"

But they cut you off mid-sentence with a knowing smile and respond, "Nice to meet you. Friends call me Life."

And there it is.

The name hits you like a quiet revelation. Life—unpredictable, fierce, the greatest rival—and the ultimate teacher. Suddenly, the tension vanished. The competition fades, and peace settles in.

You see it now: this was never just a game. Never just about winning or losing.

This mulligan—this sacred second chance—comes with one rule:

GOLDEN MULLIGAN

You can't play the same way. If you do, you'll lose again.
So, this time, you choose differently. You choose purpose.
You choose wisdom. You choose intention.
Because now, you and Life have reached an understanding. And you're not about to waste your golden mulligan.

THE FRONT NINE

CHAPTER 1
Course Management—Presence Over Perfection 101

You and Life begin tracing your steps back to the moment it all changed—the detour that rerouted your path. It's not easy. Revisiting that moment, that version of you, can be uncomfortable. But to reset the game, you must understand what took you off course.

The reset isn't instant. It's a process. A reckoning. A reconstruction. Unlike games with clear rules, this one demands your personal strategy—crafted by reflection, humility and courage. And while Life now walks beside you, not against you, Life still expects effort. Resets are honored, but never effortless. It's not for the faint of heart or the one who taps out when things get difficult. The hardest part? Finding the exact moment things shifted. Sometimes, it's obvious—a decision, a turning point, a loss, or an offense. Other times it's subtle—a slow drift. Either way, if you can face that moment honestly, your reset becomes meaningful.

GOLDEN MULLIGAN

> *As you and Life start walking the course, you notice that the landscape is breathtaking. The grass is meticulously groomed. The fairway is nonjudgmental and welcoming to all. The bunkers are intimidating yet oddly inviting. It all feels intentional—like even nature is rooting for your reset. You start thinking about how you will set up for a great swing when you find the exact place you need to reset the game. Moreover, you know your foundation must be solid. That's when your thoughts carry you to childhood.*

I used to hate golf.

There, I said it.

As a kid, it interrupted my highly anticipated Saturday morning cartoons. After five straight days of school and homework, all I wanted to do was to disappear into my cartoon lineup. Those animated characters with big personalities, catchy theme songs, and endless adventures made the weekend come alive.

Those days were carefree, filled with curiosity, imagination, and the kind of happiness you could feel vicariously through the television screen. They were the best! Back then, the last thing I wanted was to hear someone talking about a game I knew nothing about—or cared anything about, for that matter. I had my own agenda: a bowl of cereal, comfy pajamas, and a television that filled me with wonder and joy.

For me, Saturdays brought happiness, laughter, and—now that I think about it—priceless lessons. Lessons like how to avoid painted tunnels on walls—especially if you're a mouse—*everything isn't*

CHAPTER 1: COURSE MANAGEMENT—PRESENCE OVER PERFECTION

always as it appears; friends who collaborate and fight for justice as a mighty force aren't simply acquaintances—they're *Super Friends—you're inner circle matters, especially during a time of crisis*; and anyone can solve mysteries—even dogs—*so never underestimate anyone…or anything.*

But every now and then, right as I was settling in, I'd hear my father's deep voice echo through the house, rallying his friends for a tee time, "Let's go hit some balls!" he'd shout. And his pure, unadulterated joy and enthusiasm for the game could be felt in every corner of the house. Gosh, he loved him some golf!

Meanwhile, I loathed it! Every bit of it.

Truthfully, I didn't like golf for a long time. It felt like a boring interruption to whatever I had going on, especially when my father watched golf tournaments for hours. I couldn't understand how he found it so fascinating. For many years, I thought golf was the most pointless, mundane game on earth. Yet it's interesting how that same nuisance became one of the richest legacies my father has passed on to me.

My dad, a southern soul in a northern city, carried his inherited values and quiet strength from Mississippi to Michigan soon after graduating high school. He worked in a factory, and later night shifts at elementary schools. He took on whatever ad hoc jobs he could find to support his family the best way he knew how. Even on fumes, he showed up—for everyone. I am in awe of my father's tenacity, and humble strength that can't be taught—only lived. I can't fully describe it, because it speaks louder than words. I'm grateful to have witnessed it up close and honored to carry a piece of it within me.

Like everyone's journey, there were periods of uncertainty. I can remember some of the times I spent with my daddy as a little girl, not realizing those were moments when he was laid off and figuring out the next chapter. He'd put a little hat on my head, and off we'd go. We might end up at his friends' home or spend time together at ours. Other times, he'd drop me off at my grandparents' home until my mother got off work. I'm sure this was tough for him because he is and has always been a prideful provider.

Even now, my dad still apologizes for those moments. But I've told him, "We all have things we wish we could've done differently. Our mistakes and missteps don't define us." As parents, we often carry the weight of wanting to handle things better. I know that firsthand. As a young mother, my daughters had to walk with me through my own journey of growth and self-discovery. What I've come to understand is this: when we're in survival mode, we sometimes cling to things—habits, people, distractions, anything that helps us cope. They may not reflect our best selves, and some of those choices we're not proud of. But they're part of our story—not the whole book. We all have chapters we'd rewrite. What matters is how we keep writing. And my story is filled with countless chapters that serve as a testament to my father's loyalty, unconditional love, strength, and sacrifice.

As a black man raising three kids in the '70s while also navigating my mother's mental illness, I can only imagine the struggles and obstacles he faced. And yet, my father stayed present. I'm glad even now, he's still writing a beautiful narrative of wisdom I continue to cherish and learn from. Now I understand why my daddy yearned to play golf every chance he got. Golf taught my father more than hitting a ball. It taught him patience, strategy, and grace. And without knowing it, he passed those lessons on to his entire family.

Now, I adore golf. I'm hooked. What started out as a drudgery is now a delight. Playing golf is one of my favorite pastimes. But you know what would be really cool? Having a caddie. Caddies play an instrumental role. Caddies not only carry clubs, but they are also trusted advisors and strategists. Their presence can make the difference between a good and a bad round of golf. My father understood this concept well because he is a real-life caddie. My father carried more than clubs on the golf course—he carried emotional weight. He never asked for it, but he never dropped it. He bent, but didn't break. And even when he didn't know the way, he still showed up for everyone with patience, perspective, partnership, and prayers.

In many ways, I became just like him. I became the fixer. The one people come to for advice. The one carrying too much. These days, I still fight the urge to correct everything. Maybe it's a trauma response—or my arch-nemesis, perfectionism. I also try to guard my tongue when it comes to correcting others, especially when I really need to focus on addressing my own issues and shortcomings. I'm working hard on improving these areas of opportunity for me because I'm learning: my work isn't in fixing—

it's in *being*. And one of the greatest lessons my father taught me wasn't about perfection or performance; it was about presence.

Turns out, golf was always teaching us both that life doesn't always give you a perfect setup. Sometimes the wind shifts, the terrain gets tricky, and even when you're doing your best—things don't always go as planned. But I watched my father handle those moments with quiet resolve. And that little girl tagging along with her daddy with a little hat on her head? She was taking notes. I learned to play through life's challenges with resilience, heart, strategy, and strength. I didn't know it back then, but every round of setbacks, every hard season, every quiet win was preparing me. Teaching me how to read the green, adjust my stance, recover from a bad shot, and most of all keep showing up fully present, even when the path ahead is unclear. Just like my daddy then—and still does now.

Presence over perfection 101. That was my first real lesson in course management.

CHAPTER 2

Some Rescues Are Rough

As you and Life continue walking, you start to feel like you will never find the right place for the reset. You start to feel weak, and Life notices you moving slowly—possibly away from your goal. Life sees you fading. You're tired, disoriented, and you cry out, "Jesus!" Life has an immediate knee-jerk reaction and gives you that look—you know the one. A mother's "Don't come to the Lord with that ungrateful attitude" look. Then, Life regroups, points off into the distance, and gently whispers, "Let's make it to that tree." You look up and see a big tree with wide branches and plenty of shade just above a hill. For some reason even though you are looking up and over the hill, the hill isn't obstructing the view. Life continues, "If you look to the hills, you can see it. Let's rest for a while and take a load off." Life sounded as if they were confident sitting under a tree of all things would help you in any way. However, you trusted Life's instincts and obliged.

The infamous rough in golf—thick, wild, and unforgiving—is where balls (and sometimes dignity) go to hide. The area of longer and thicker grass that borders a fairway, designed to make shots more challenging and difficult. One bad swing, and suddenly you're knee-deep in frustration. Tempted to lash out or swing wildly, ironically, to feel some sense of control. Kind of like life, right? But golf, in its own unique way, teaches you to pause, breathe, and think. You stop blaming the grass and start strategizing.

Golf became more than a game for me—it became a teacher. A true test of spiritual disciplines. You can practice, prepare, and still find yourself stuck. But that's where patience is refined. Presence becomes powerful. And prayer? That's when it becomes real.

I learned that from my mother.

Her answer when things got tough and rough, "Take it to the Lord in prayer." No matter how much I vented about my problems (and I could go on), she always listened. Then, with a calm disposition, steady voice, and limitless faith she'd offer a gentle reminder to *take it to the Lord in prayer*.

My mother shaped my mindset early on and taught me to lean not on my own understanding, but to cast my burdens on the Lord whenever things didn't go as planned. She instilled in me to have the faith to believe that with Him, all things are possible, and the perseverance to press forward knowing everything will work out, regardless of my circumstances.

That simple, profound instruction became my strength when I needed it most. It renewed and restored my faith and nurtured a deep trust in a divine plan that grounded me when I couldn't find my way.

That same mindset easily translates to golf and resonates with me every time I step on the course.

My mother was a poised and faith-filled woman who embodied grace. A secretary by trade, her typewriting speed and shorthand precision left my brother, sister, and me in awe. I can still picture her at the kitchen table, fingers gliding across keys, the rhythmic tap ringing in my ears. My favorite part was watching the carriage on the typewriter glide back into place with each new line—followed by that familiar high-pitched *ding* that still echoes in my mind.

My mother absolutely adored her children. She would always embrace my brother with a big grin and say, "Mommy's only boy." My brother cherished those priceless moments, soaking up their special bond as he rubbed his cheeks against her soft, golf-ball-sized cheeks and held her tight. You could see their unbreakable bond in his eyes—it was the kind of love that spoke louder than words.

My mother's sharp skills and professionalism fascinated my sister and me—we wanted to be just like her. We also embraced many of the hobbies she loved and introduced us to. We joined the church choir. We took home economics where we learned how to sew and bake, and studied piano and secretarial classes at school for several years. In fact, I landed my first job in a corporate environment as a result of my secretarial (block) co-op class in high school. I was 16 years old, earning my own money—thought I was doing something. My sister followed in my mother's footsteps with a similar experience. I'm not sure if I was trying to be like my big sister or my mother, but I admired them both—and I was watching, learning, and growing.

I learned to type fast, work fast, and move fast. However, no one really emphasized how important it is to rest. I really believe I could've benefited from a class focused on restoration. I can see it now: The Academy of Restoration, a place where you come to take a nap…or perhaps reflect and practice mindfulness. I can't help but chuckle silently to myself because I can hear my big brother and sister tell me to go to *that* class in their own special way. It may not be what you're thinking though. They would probably tell me a little more like this, "Go sit your tail down somewhere. What's that class called again? Academy something —you need to go there." Yep, that sounds like something my brother or sister would tell me if I were moving too fast, which would be often. Maybe, just maybe, bringing back naptime from kindergarten through high school would've been the genius move we all needed—teachers included. It might have helped us restless teenage souls perform differently. Who knows? But as they say, hindsight is 20/20.

Having said that, I should also mention there was one class I got permission to fall asleep in. Drama class. Our drama teacher would tell us in her distinct theatrical way to imagine a bright and warm ball traveling up and down your body, releasing tension in our muscles. My brain was way too active for that. Sometimes I would peek out my eye to see what other students were doing. I'm not nosey though. I like to think I've always been blessed with a high sense of curiosity, the kind that sneaks out of my left eye sometimes. You know—that whole *keep one eye open* idiom we practice without even realizing it. Fortunately, and possibly not by happenstance I would eventually fall asleep, and it was the best sleep ever! I was probably tired and didn't sit still long enough to recalibrate my body, mind, and soul—even for the sake of a holistic equilibrium. That class was needed more than I knew.

Looking back, I still can't believe I was sleeping in class without any repercussions. Drama class was fun yet purposeful. Those improvs sharpened my ability to think on my feet—my wit, humor, and charm flourished—and my body surrendered to a spirit of inner peace it had been craving. And sometimes, in that peace, I rested.

One thing I can say about my mother is that she learned the value of rest. After her career as a secretary ended due to health reasons, she spent more time slowing down, reflecting, and simply being still. I believe she also learned to lean on her support system—and on God's word—trusting His wisdom instead of her own understanding more than ever. Her faith was strong, unwavering, and deeply rooted. She instilled that same powerful faith-driven purpose in us, as her children, which is the greatest gift my mother gave me.

It showed up in those familiar Bible scriptures my sister, brother, and I—and later, our children—would read or recite to my mother at a moment's notice. If my mother pulled out her Bible, you already knew what to do and we would stop whatever we were doing to honor of her wishes. I'll admit. I never quite appreciated the "wine is a mocker…" verse since I didn't drink like that or at all as a child, but I never would have said that to my mother. I understood her intentions.

Her consistency in how she raised us was clear. She wanted to make sure we stayed rooted in faith and close to the church. And even if we wandered, we always knew how to find our way back. Her spiritually led, empowering words always had a way of guiding us home. I thank my mother today for grounding us in faith—a foundation that still carries me through life's rough terrain.

What I did not grasp as a child and into my teenage years was that my mother also carried an invisible burden—mental illness. I'm not a physician, but I wonder when her mental state became ill. It still baffles me, because I've always cherished the moments when my mother's actions reflected deep commitment to family and faith—in ways both beautiful and sound-minded.

My mother's illness would sporadically surface, unpredictable, and sometimes after many years had passed without any warning. As a family, we tried to help my mother to the best of our untrained ability—at home and in clinical settings. We did what we could—guided by love, not expertise, as her mind wrestled with battles she fought quietly within.

As a child, I could not fully understand how my mother's mental illness shaped our home and a lasting dynamic, but it did. We bonded together as a close-knit family grounded in unconditional love. No matter the circumstances. No matter the distance. No matter the obstacles. My father, mother, sister, brother, grandfather, and I had a bond that no one or nothing could break. We may have disagreements, but we would inevitably come back together stronger than ever. Our capacity for compassion and empathy grew stronger as we did our best to support my mother through her unseen battles without judgement.

Some days were harder than others, but my mother fought her *disease* within showing up with as much strength and grace as she could. Even as she battled with a mental burden, she recharged through faith, music, and sacred pauses. Her faith was her anchor. I didn't have the language back then to name what I saw—but I knew love when I saw it. I knew faith when I saw it because she lived it out loud. Those early caregiving experiences gave me a deep understanding of faith, trauma and adversity all at once.

Even as a young child, I sensed more than I could explain. That awareness shaped my desire to help others in their time of need, with grace, humility, and sensitivity guiding how I care. I often give a gentle disclaimer; however, "I'm ministering to myself too." It's my way of admitting that if I ever sound like I don't practice what I preach, it's only because I'm still a work in progress myself.

Oh, the hypocrisy, some might say—and that's a fair argument. At times, it can appear hypocritical. In other moments, it's simply misunderstood, and credibility feels compromised. But here's a paradigm shift I'd like to offer: sometimes we have to encourage ourselves. We must speak light and life into circumstances, even when knowing better and doing better aren't yet aligned.

Now I see that I wasn't only ministering to every version of myself that endured hardships and trauma; I was also speaking life into my inner child and rewriting the narrative and imprint traumatic experiences left behind even if I didn't want to follow my own advice sometimes.

The beautiful thing about revelations is they often come hand in hand with rescues. Whether they reveal the root cause, the cost, the lesson behind the chaos, or serve as a catalyst to healing trauma. There's almost always something to be gleaned.

Some rescues come gently. Others come after you've cried out, broken down, or collapsed under the weight of what you were never meant to carry alone. If you've ever found yourself in life's rough, confused exhausted, or just plain lost—you are not alone. Maybe you've had to hold it all together for everyone else. Maybe you've been the quiet strength in the middle of chaos, or the one who loved someone through a kind of pain that didn't have a name you were familiar with. I see you. I am you. You are not alone.

For me, golf has become a masterclass in handling, trauma and burdens too heavy to carry at times. Like golf, there will be rough days in life. Situations you didn't ask for and can't control. But you can control how you respond. Golf has helped me manage my reactions and responses. It's taught me to embrace disappointments as an essential part of growth, not a sign of defeat. It helped me breathe and rest in knowing every missed shot is an opportunity to reset, refocus, and rise stronger.

In the end, golf has taught me that rescues aren't always dramatic. Sometimes you save a ball right on the edge of deep waters—gentle, steady, and intentional. And in life—it's the same. With patience, prayer, and the divine wisdom only He can impart, you will find your way back into play.

My mother taught me many things, but her most enduring lesson would last me a lifetime. I still hear voice her saying, "Take it to the Lord in prayer." And somehow, in ways I can't always explain, grace shows up right on time—every time.

And that's what an unmatched rescue looks like for me.

CHAPTER 3

Greens, Cornbread, and a Dash of Hot Sauce

The putting green in golf is an area of short grass that surrounds the pin. It's designed for putting the golf ball into the hole with finesse. Some call it "the greens." Back in the day, lots of people called money "green." But for me, "greens" are memories—of family, faith, stability, trust, and nourishment in every form. I grew up surrounded by them—rolling around on manicured lawns, at the dinner table, and in the hearts of my maternal grandparents.

Growing up, the best days included crabapple fights, bikes, skateboarding, and cheering from the sidelines while the fast kids raced like Olympic hopefuls. Me? I couldn't run fast to save my life, but I could dream. Big. And most of my dreams came true when I visited my grandparents' house.

Their home was a world of its own—bold, beautiful, and sacred. Walking in felt like stepping onto the set of the Jeffersons—

everything was meticulous and shining. My grandmother glided through her home in caftans that whispered elegance, and her jewelry gleamed like it had its own light source. Even the bathroom had matching curtains and fringe. Nothing was random. Everything had purpose. But it wasn't just about appearances. Their home was a museum of memories, a boot camp of discipline, and a sanctuary of love. You had to act like you had some sense there.

My grandmother was grace and grit. Her presence could quiet a room without any words. And when she said, "You better eat all of it," while handing me a bowl of orange sherbet, I knew it wasn't a suggestion. Even dessert came with expectations. Standards were high, perhaps a quiet echo of generations who always expected more from themselves.

She was one of the first Black women to start and retire from General Motors. An Arkansas-born visionary who made her way to Philadelphia and then Michigan. Her story wasn't handed to her—it was earned. She was proud and powerful in her own right. Given the era, I'm sure she overcame adversity as she accomplished her goals and relentlessly pursued her own definition of success. And her life experiences may have shaped her philosophy when it came to child-rearing. She didn't play. And though her methods could be strict (let's just say my generation might recall what it meant to pick your own switch), her love was real. I never doubted it.

> *Wouldn't you know it—just as you're navigating the course with Life, the rain starts to fall. You approach a bunker that looks suspiciously like cornbread, golden and crumbly with grains that seem baked by the sun. Life eyes the sand trap but decides it's not worth the struggle. You look at Life, smile, and think to yourself, some dread these traps. But to you? It's just cornbread. You go with the flow, because you've learned that the same rain that nourishes the greens can, in its own way, nourish the sand too.*

Now, let's talk about that cornbread.

Mmm, mmm, mmm... golden brown with crispy edges and a soft center. My grandmother's cornbread was the kind of food that made you close your eyes and hum. Every time, it was perfect and that kind of consistency wasn't just culinary—it was emotional. Her love was baked into every bite. My grandmother didn't say "I love you" often, but we felt it—in the meals, in the structure, in the way she showed up. She didn't just raise her kids—she raised the standard.

Dinner was like clockwork. My grandfather came home from work, and the dinner table was already set. Sometimes with the fine china dinnerware pieces I was blessed to inherit. My grandmother would always tell us not to bother my grandfather after a long day of work, but kids don't follow instructions well when a "King" walks through the door. We'd sneak to the door or sometimes run to it, knowing he was going to give us a big hug. We also had a hunch that he would save us from a switch ready to handle our disobedience, if my grandmother felt so inclined to tap our hard-headed behind. Fortunately, the king of the house would whisper something to my grandmother, and the next thing we knew, we were off to our uncle's store for candy just like that. My uncle who owned the store happened to be my grandmother's brother, so I guess she was okay with our tasty commitment to supporting a black-owned business —and family.

Needless to say, my grandfather had this magical ability to soften my grandmother's steel—not by overpowering, but by understanding her. That's real strength. Although my grandmother was a leader by far and set the tone of the house, my grandfather led her heart as he navigated his role with love. My grandfather ultimately led the entire family line by example rooted in unconditional love. Their home was a safe space for me before I even knew what that phrase meant. After my grandmother transitioned, my safe space later became known as "Granddaddy's House." My grandfather was my second daddy. My real-life king. Yes, he was actually a King! He was cut from a cloth woven with the highest fiber of manhood that's not easy to find nowadays. He was the kind of man who could fix a motor and a mood. He taught us how to fish, help our neighbors, mind our business, and handle it too. His house was a gathering spot where free bottles of Coca-Cola and good vibes flowed.

Today, I understand why his royal name mattered. He didn't just wear it—he earned it. His life was a quiet testimony. He didn't need a spotlight because he carried his light with him. Everyone knew my grandfather as Mr. King. Never mind the fact that "King" was his last name. He was also known as "The Giver," the neighborhood mechanic, the "Go-To," and any other title synonymous with a friend you can count on. He helped everyone. Young and old. If you needed a tool, a ride, a dollar, or a word—he had it.

Children brought their bicycles to him for repairs as if they were pulling into the service lane at a dealership. My grandfather didn't just raise his kids and grandkids—he helped raise the community. His generosity knew no bounds. He had plenty of time on his hands after retiring from the factory in his 50s—like my grandmother did—and I love that he chose to use those same hands to serve others as the days passed. I recall riding with him many times in the back seat of his car as he gave rides to friends and family, running errands and lending a helping hand wherever he could. I also loved riding in his motorboat and camper—both matched his white and blue house perfectly. My brother, sister, and I even had our own matching fancy fishing poles. We'd take them on fishing trips to a nearby park with our friends, laughing and competing to see who could catch the biggest fish.

My grandfather took us on all kinds of adventures—swimming, shopping, amusements parks, restaurants, skating rinks, and even parties. No matter where we went, he always made sure we got there and back safely. And when we got old enough to drive, he made sure we had our own transportation—even mopeds. My brother had two, and he would style and profile on them—matching helmets and all. It was really cool seeing a sea of flashy mopeds outside of my grandfather's home; knowing my own brother was among them. It was fun. That is, until he crashed one—

CHAPTER 3: GREENS, CORNBREAD, AND A DASH OF HOT SAUCE

or someone else did—okay me, but you get the point. Then my grandfather would find out and that's when fun turned to fury.

My grandfather wasn't perfect—like a dash of hot sauce, his tongue was a little spicy if you upset him—but he was steady, strong, and full of care. He was like my grandmother in a sense—he didn't play either—but he was more of an observer. He'd silently watch and listen, then tell you exactly how he felt about someone or something, especially if it rubbed him the wrong way.

We always knew it was coming "That ain't NOTHING!" he'd passionately say whenever he was in full disagreement. We'd laugh, but deep down, we always knew he was right.

Needless to say, my grandfather gave freely, without expecting anything in return—unless you borrowed it. Then he'd talk about you if you didn't pay it back. But he'd still help you because everything he did came from a place of love, not judgment. He prided himself on being a man of his word and expected the same from others.

Sometimes I worried that he poured so much into everyone, there was little left for himself as he aged. Then one day, I shared those thoughts with someone, and they asked me one question that turned my world upside down—in a good way. It softened my heart and helped settle into the final stage of grief: acceptance.

She asked me, "How do you know he wasn't satisfied with giving whatever he could?" Then she added, "Maybe it fulfilled him." I sat there speechless—no words. It was an immediate paradigm shift. For the first time, I considered another possibility" maybe giving in any way he could, regardless of the outcome didn't empty him. His intentions were always pure, and if he knew someone needed help, his heart always acted. Her argument was something I couldn't debate from my one-sided vantage point, so I received it.

Looking back, I see how deeply his identity was tied to service. It was in his bones. Up until the graceful age of 97 years old, he was still giving advice, help, unconditional love, and support.

His mantra was simple: Keep going. And it wasn't just words—it was how he lived his life for 97 years. I deeply admire my grandfather's strength to withstand life's ebbs and flows while still showing up as a beacon of light. To do so for that length of time is nothing short of remarkable. Some of us can barely endure life's ups and downs for 97 days, let alone 97 years.

That's what community is all about. You don't serve others seeking anything in return. You partner with others for a common cause and the greater good. You hold space for them when you have the capacity to do so. You care. That's what I remember most about my grandfather. He cared enough to help others, and I'm blessed to have experienced his goodwill firsthand.

CHAPTER 3: GREENS, CORNBREAD, AND A DASH OF HOT SAUCE

> *You and Life press on through the rain. There wasn't a cloud in sight—the sun still beams above, warm and steady, while the rain falls cool and light, as if it were watering something deep inside you. You pause as Life takes a sip of water, then you tilt your head toward the sky, marveling at the strange harmony of sunshine and rain working together. You raise your bottle in a silent toast—not only to the mission ahead, but for Life's steadfast companionship. Life has chosen to walk beside you, pursuing the perfect spot for your mulligan reset. As Life speaks positive words of affirmation that nourishes your soul, you can appreciate the rain's nourishment to the course.*

The seed was planted, and I went on to serve communities locally and internationally. I'm grateful my grandfather modeled what a servant leader looks like. He greatly influenced the humanitarian path and perspective in me—and his legacy lives on in the hearts of everyone in our family and beyond. What an incredible footprint to leave behind—far more precious than that monetary *green* paper my granddaddy had plenty of when I was younger. Because generational wealth, to me, has always meant more than money.

After my grandfather transitioned, I came to the realization that grief doesn't always roar. Sometimes, it slowly exhales and quietly shows up as gratitude—even on the fairway—because grieving a perfect swing that went awry doesn't seem fair when you're so close to your goal. But you're still in the game—and that alone is a blessing.

I'm learning to say, "Thank You" for the memories, for the example, for the seed planted in me that transforms grief into gratitude. Plus, my grandfather kept going and encouraged me to do the same. No matter the circumstances.

I just had to bring up cornbread, didn't I? I digress, but my mouth still waters whenever I think about my grandmother's cornbread. It's funny how memories can rise sometimes like rainwater on the fairway—shimmering, nourishing, and glistening…like butter melting on top of cornbread.

Now that I think about it, there's plenty of green grass on the fairway—and it comes in a variety of rich hues. It's beautiful. But in contrast, there are also bunkers—a strategically placed hazard—a sunken and depressed area containing sand, otherwise known as a sand trap. On the course of life, I came across sand traps that look like setbacks. But I had to remind myself, it's really just cornbread in disguise. I've been here before. I'll find my way through.

Because my grandfather taught me how.

So, I keep going.

Just like Granddaddy said.

CHAPTER 4

The Breaks

The rain stopped when you made it to the green on the fourteenth hole. Life lifted the flag as an invitation to practice putting. You bend down to stretch and started tapping your feet. You rocked heel to toe reading the surface like an old-school boombox had just dropped a beat. You started out searching for a hidden curvature or slope that causes the golf ball to change direction as it rolls toward the hole—otherwise known as the "break" in the golfing world. Suddenly, you remembered a perfect putt that curved right and dropped into the hole on the most challenging course you've ever played. There's something about that flawless putt that makes you want to break out into a celebratory dance every time you remember it.

Life did a double take as you moonwalked but didn't say anything. Life just raised a suspicious eyebrow, remained quiet, and let you flow. Then you started twisting and popping like you traveled back in time to a breakdancing battle in the '80s. Breaking every unwritten rule of golf because sometimes the best way to honor where you are is to remember where you've been. And back then? You were carried by a village.

Aaah. The '80s. What an era. Often imitated, never duplicated. Back in those days, I bounced between the Southside and Westside of my hometown like I had dual citizenship. I did! I was welcomed with open arms in both communities. And both sides of town understood the customary, routine assignment. Always stay ready for a battle. Rap and breakdancing, that is. And make sure your crew has your back.

My crew? We laughed, danced, and had pure, unadulterated fun. Thick skin was mandatory but love always underscored our jokes. Well, most of the time. Either way, laughter and good times were the cornerstone of our village. And our village was deep. Familial elders, siblings, cousins, neighbors, mentors, honorary big brothers, and sisters poured into us in ways we didn't understand until later. This village, our community, gave me rhythm, resilience, and real joy. And breakdancing was our universal language. No matter which block you hailed from, you understood every spin, pop, lock, and move, even if it was unprecedented, because it was more than performance—it was preparation. Breakdancing wasn't just something we did. It was who we were. This was our version of therapy, expression, and art—all rolled into one. We would make up routines with enough energy to dance all day long. And honestly? I wasn't even the best one. But I had heart—and a good beat was all I needed. I still love a good beat, no matter the genre of music today. Oh, and chances are, I'll break out into a dance—no matter where I am.

The '80s were rebellious and unconventional in the best way. Everywhere you looked, you saw art. Graffiti, asymmetrical haircuts, bamboo earrings, spotless sneakers, colored Levi's, Run-DMC and LL Cool J inspired outfits, and don't even get me started on Salt-N-Pepa. Some may think I'm *pushing it* when I say elements of their style and disposition were admired and duplicated by 9 out of 10 teenage girls, but that's just my humble opinion.

By the way, MC Lyte was one of my favorites. And when it came to the grand showcase? Talent and fashion shows? I rocked both stages with creativity, confidence, and style.

I didn't just survive that era—I was shaped by it. Every break I experienced on a cardboard floor was a metaphor for the ones I'd meet later in life. The unexpected shifts. The need to read the room and respond accordingly. The community we had to lean on when things felt offbeat that embodied the kind of loyalty you can't manufacture. It might not be blood, but it's born and built to last a lifetime.

What I remember most about my village is how they prepared me for a pivotal stage in my life—the one I stepped onto willingly—my personal stage built just for me. It was there that my curiosity was nurtured, my mindset was reshaped, and I was transformed into a lifelong learner. This quintessential stage was cultivated, above all, in school.

High School was my safe haven. I shined and found my rhythm without missing a beat—socially, academically, and in leadership. I've always loved to learn and still yearn to grow more each day. Back then, I joined clubs, organizations, and soaked up wisdom from mentors who helped cultivate a sense of pride and purpose deep within me. I learned valuable lessons about life, friendship, and finding my place in the world.

Decades later, when my life hit its most terrifying "break"—a health crisis that shook me to the core—like a scratch on your favorite record—my village showed up again. Old friends, new friends, colleagues, family members, neighbors, Sorors, Divine Nine brothers and sisters, former classmates—everyone rallied. They didn't wait to be asked. They just showed up. With prayers. With presence. With love.

Of course, my family was front and center. Covering me, holding me up when I couldn't stand, reminding me I still had purpose—even on days when I didn't feel like myself. I leaned on their strength and my faith. And deep down, I remembered the rhythm—the same one felt in organizations with open doors, high school corridors—and of course—on those cardboard breakdancing floors. The beat of life may change, but whether it's fast or slow keep dancing, keep moving, and don't give up.

Looking back, I realized I was being trained. Every breakdancing routine, every leadership role, every neighborhood hangout—it all built me. When I started college and stepped into motherhood before I earned a degree, it wasn't easy. But I kept going—with grit and faith.

My village didn't just raise me. They carried me. Corrected me. Covered me. And strategically danced with me along the way. Some people saw something in me I didn't fully recognize yet. And nurtured it. That special and unique essence one of my confidants refers to as my "je ne sais quoi." My village gave me perspective, polish, and protection I didn't know would translate into wherewithal, tenacity, and demure later in life.. They clapped for me—even when life didn't. They helped prepare me for the next chapter, the following one, and the current one. That's what a solid support system looks like. And my village is *Solid Gold* personified!

They say it takes a village to raise a child. I say it takes a village to hold up adults too—especially when life throws us curves. Because the truth is that life doesn't always move in straight lines. It swerves. It breaks. And sometimes we drop the ball and everything goes left. But if you've learned to read the breaks—and you've got people in your corner who've seen you spin before and still believe you'll land on your feet—you'll be just fine.

So now, when I'm on the green and my putt breaks left or right, I smile. Because my village and I learned how to turn every single step backwards into a step forward. We understand the code that breaks the mold. Even if we have to slow dance, two-step, or stand firm, remarkably balanced upside down—on one hand, we are still moving forward. Like a centipede's feet—each step small on its own, but together creating unstoppable motion.

…And these are the breaks.

CHAPTER 5

Stats, Handicaps, and Hats

> *After stretching, Life pulled out a scorecard and started scanning the numbers, eyes narrowing. Then Life looked up and asked, "So, what's your handicap?" You paused—not because you didn't know the answer, but because you were curious where Life was going with this conversation. In golf, statistics—or "stats"—matter. They measure accuracy, distance, performance under pressure, where to place you, and who to place you with. But in life, statistics can be misleading. They box us in. Label us. Reduce our complexity to a percentage or a predicted outcome.*

By the stats, I should have struggled in a multiplicity of ways. In the '90s I became a college student at 17, welcomed my first daughter at 19 and by 23 I had my second daughter. The statistics about teenage mothers rarely paint a promising picture, but some stories can't be summed up in numbers. Mine was one of them.

I never referred to myself as a "teenage mother." I was simply a mother. Young, yes. Imperfect, certainly. But determined, loving, and doing my best. Though some days the best I could offer came with collateral lessons and my daughters experienced them alongside me. And while I've made mistakes, I've also built a life I'm proud of. My daughters are educated, resilient, and compassionate women. And now, I parent with more listening, more space, more trust in God's timing and guidance rather than my own. Particularly when He instructs me to *be still…and know.*

Looking back, there are things I wish I had done differently. Not out of shame, but because wisdom has since walked through the doors that immaturity once kicked open. Still, my love for my daughters has always been the kind that transcends numbers and moments. My daughters are adults now. Like myself, they are human, and my daughters have experienced both highs and lows like most human beings. But God's grace and mercy have kept them through it all.

Stepping back is never easy. Especially when your instinct is to shield, solve problems, and soften the blows of life before they land. But I trust that God's plan for them—like His plan for me—was written long before I tried to control the story. I am learning to mother them differently. No longer just as a protector, but as a partner. Not just with answers, but with space to listen and support them as they navigate their own lives.

Motherhood doesn't come with a scorecard. If it did, most of us would ignore it anyway. Because how do you quantify the first time they said, "Mommy?" The nights you didn't sleep because they were sick or sad? The joy when they succeed? The guilt when you fall short? I don't have time to tally sacrifices or mark wins and losses. But if I did, I'd do it all over again. Maybe wiser, more aware, more grounded—but with the same love. In my opinion, there are no birdies or bogeys to count in parenting—just lessons, love, and moments that matter.

So today, when I find myself in life's bunkers or facing a long, uncertain shot, I remind myself: I've come back from worse. I've played through pain. And I've learned that sometimes the best rounds aren't the ones where everything goes right—they're the ones where you find the courage to keep swinging when everything goes wrong. While others may track your hazards and handicaps, you understand that neither calculation could measure your heart or the brilliance of your brain—one that refuses to be defined by numbers.

Speaking of the brain—if you really want to talk statistics, then let's talk about miracles.

I'm a stroke survivor who underwent emergency surgery on the left side of my brain last year. That title alone comes packed with numbers, probabilities, and outcomes medical professionals and hospital visitors whisper about. Words like handicap and limitations tend to follow stroke survivors like shadows. According to every chart, every onlooker's cautious tone, I wasn't supposed to bounce back like this. So, if we're measuring miracles, measure this:

Faith that wouldn't let go.

A mind that rewired itself to remember who I am, and the limitless possibilities God placed within me.

CHAPTER 5: STATS, HANDICAPS, AND HATS

A body that didn't just recover—it rose.

And a spirit that didn't just survive—it soared.

Some people see "teenage mother" or "stroke survivor" and immediately think "statistic." A handicap. An obstacle to dreams. But here I am—living life, loving golf, and enjoying the fruits of my labor. I could add a few more labels—divorcée, compassionate caregiver, manager, entrepreneur, coach, mentor, sister, daughter, mother (my favorite), comeback queen—you get the point. I've worn many hats in my lifetime: some handed to me, some I chose, and others I had to stitch back together just to keep going. Each one tells a story—of survival, strength, and showing up even when life tried to count me out. But none of them ever defined me. I defined how I wore them. Each one is a badge—not of brokenness, but of boldness.

If my life were a billboard for every young mother, or anyone who was ever doubted or been dismissed because of a label they refuse to wear—the caption would read:

~~STATS, HANDICAPS, & HATS~~
You define them and how you choose to wear them.

Lots of people keep score in this game called life—tracking every win and every loss. But I've learned to play differently. I strike through labels and redefine them. I play with heart. With faith, with a God-given resilience that can't be measured—or contained— by any label.

> *So, when Life asked, "What's your handicap?" You just smiled. Depends on how one defines it. Because the only thing your handicap measures now... is the distance you've already come. And you can't track that on any scorecard.*

Let them count stats.

Let them debate outcomes.

I'll be right here—living proof that God has the final say, and that miracles outshine the odds every day.

> *You wiped the sweat off your forehead and placed the visor back in position—not to shield you from the sun, but as a quiet salute to all the storms you've weathered. A gentle reminder of the light your unique life experiences bring to the game. And it shines no matter the forecast. That's why you always wear your hats with pride.*

CHAPTER 6

Hazards, Hooks, and Healing

Every golf course has its hazards. Most are marked on the map—predictable and visible. Some golfers consider a dramatic hook on a hole that curves to avoid a hazard or obstacle marked on the map.

Other hazards appear out of nowhere, catching you off guard just when you think you're finally finding your rhythm. Life is no different.

Having a stroke was one of those unmarked hazards. No warning. No signs. One day, I was on a golf course taking pictures for an outing— balancing life, pursuing goals, and motherhood. The next day everything went quiet, still, and terrifying.

Prior to that moment, I was showing up for others, managing a career, fulfilling entrepreneurial and personal obligations, and pushing through fatigue—until my body said, "Enough." My swing, my stride, my speech, my steps—all of it slipped out of my control in an instant. I was in the rough, and not the kind you recover from with a quick fix. I had veered into a place I didn't recognize. A true "out-of-bounds", unfamiliar moment.

In those first couple of hours as I suffered my stroke, even the strongest part of me was shaken and disoriented. I couldn't find words. I couldn't type a sentence. I couldn't move like I used to. Physically and mentally I was in a space I didn't recognize, and honestly, didn't understand how to accept.

But if life had taught me anything up to that point, it was this: you don't mentally concede the hole—you play it out.

So I did.

At first, healing looked like resting when I didn't want to, asking for help when I didn't know how, and showing up to physical therapy with nothing but determination and a quiet prayer. It looked like learning to hold a fork again without it slipping out of my hand. It looked like avoiding burns and pain on my right side because my sensory nerves were damaged, and I couldn't feel when things were too hot or too cold. I only felt pain. It looked like I was slowly finding words to express my thoughts. And then, one day, it looked like holding a golf club again. And I'm right-handed, y'all! Hallelujah!

That moment was sacred—not because I swung with power, but because I swung with hope.

Initially, it felt like I had lost everything that made me "me." The words I used to type with purpose didn't follow instructions. The energy I used to pour into others barely kept me upright. I was forced to stop, reset, and reimagine my swing at life—both literally and figuratively.

But here's what life—like golf—teaches you: every hazard presents a choice. You can panic and try to force your way out, or you can breathe, assess the lie (even the ones you whisper to yourself) and focus on making the next move from where you are in life and in the game of golf.

In those early weeks, healing felt more like surviving. I wasn't yet aiming for the green—I was just trying to gain strength on my right side and stand firmly. But with time, faith, and an army of support—I began to see that this "hazard" wasn't the end of my round. It was a sacred invitation to learn a new course. A new rhythm. A better way of living. Golf gave me the first glimpse of hope. I still recall the day I held a club again—it felt like holding a beloved piece of myself. I wasn't swinging like I used to, but I was swinging. And that was everything.

Healing didn't happen in a straight line. It curved in unexpected ways as I desperately tried to restore my equilibrium. Golfers strive to maintain balance too. In golf, when you close the clubface and hit the ball curving left (for a right-handed player) it's called a hook. Again, sometimes golfers use a hook shot on purpose to stay in play. To bypass an obstacle. Well, my obstacle, a stroke, was a little different. It wasn't marked on the course I was familiar with. The game as I knew it. It was unexpected and sudden. I lost control over my right arm and my left hand fought to get it back in play. But like a golf player who knows the game isn't played hole by hole but stroke by stroke, I started to track my post-stroke progress not by speed, but by presence. I was here. I was alive. I was still in the game—the game of life, which is the greatest game of all.

I didn't return to the game the same. I returned with a new mindset. The old me measured success by output—how much I could get done in 24 hours, how much I could give, how many goals I could check off. Conversely, the new me began to measure progress by peace *of* mind and peace *in* mind. Also, I learned to appreciate the hazards—not because they were easy, but because they revealed my strength. They taught me to listen to my body, trust my faith, and surrender to the process. They made me more patient, more compassionate, and more aligned with purpose.

I started asking better questions:

Did I honor what my body needed today?

Did I listen to my limits instead of pushing past them just to prove something?

Did I make space for rest without guilt?

The hazards of life—like a health crisis or stroke don't just slow you down. They force a reckoning. A spiritual recalibration. They ask you to trust in something deeper than routine or strength. For me, that was God. Faith became more than a word—it became my pace. My power. My peace.

CHAPTER 6: HAZARDS, HOOKS, AND HEALING

> *The rain returned, softer, as if Heaven knew both you and the course needed more cleansing before you proceeded any further. You and Life stood still beneath a wide golf umbrella Life used to cover you. You thought about all of the times an umbrella covered you during a storm or at the threat of lightening...far too many. Out in the distance, you notice the driving range and memories continue to stir. Priceless memories you can't ignore.*

In full transparency, some days, the course still intimidates me—the fairways feel too long, the stakes too high. But the driving range? That's where I found freedom. On the range, there's no scorecard. No water hazards looming over your head. For me, there's growth. One ball at a time, one breath at a time. I learned to measure my healing not by yardage, but by rhythm. Moreover, it was on the driving range where I learned how to trust my body again. And my golf coach customized my golf lessons to help me build confidence along the way! My father always told me to relax since I was a child. He also tells me to relax when we go to the driving range today. Sometimes I can hear his voice as I loosen up my muscles before I take my swing.

The driving range became my sanctuary. My peace. Here, the hazards of life—the stroke, the fear, the doubt—couldn't tee off against me. Instead, I teed up faith, I aimed at possibility, and I practiced resilience. I still carry that spirit with me to the course today, knowing my real comeback happened in those non-judgmental rows of mats and buckets of balls. Because healing, like driving, doesn't demand perfection. It demands presence and the determination to reach your destination. Steady and persistent.

And persistence is something I have in abundance—just like ball-covered grass you hit into at the driving range. On the course of life some days I still hit into the rough. My memory may falter. My muscles may become fatigued, and I rest when I need to. Then I keep moving forward not with perfection, but with presence—present for life: mind, body, and soul.

And here's the truth most people don't tell you about hazards: they don't mean you're losing—because you're still in the game.

So, when I step up to the tee box of each new day, I don't fear the water, the bunkers, the unpredictable winds, or even the hazards of life per se. I respect them—because I've been through worse. I've climbed out of deeper pits. And I've learned that healing isn't about returning to who you were—it's about embracing who you're becoming.

CHAPTER 7

Get a Grip (On Yourself)

Life recalled seeing you out on the course earlier. Your stance was steady, but your aim was off. Life smiled and said, "Mind if I share something with you?" It was a rhetorical question. Without waiting for a response, Life leaned in and quoted something often attributed to Zig Ziglar. Life whispered, "If you aim at nothing, you will hit it every time." Unbeknownst to you, Life's words would echo as a driving force from that point forward.

There's something about the fundamentals. In the world of golf some say you've got to get your G.A.S.P. right—grip, aim, stance, and posture—if you want any real shot at the green. What I didn't understand until later was how much that same principle applied to every area of my life. Relationships? Yes. Career and goals? Absolutely. Purpose and spiritual alignment? Of course. But most of all—me. Over the years, I've discovered how I grip situations, how I aim at my intentions, the stance I take when life presses me, and the posture I hold when everything feels like it's crumbling. Each choice reflects how I treat myself. At its core, it's an act of self-love. And if I'm being honest, for a long time I was holding on too tightly. There were seasons when I gripped things like a lifeline. I thought if I just held on long enough, things would turn around. Sometimes they did. Oftentimes, they didn't. And in that tension, I lost time, clarity, and peace—clinging to burdens, people, and stuff I was never meant to carry. My healing began when I loosened my grip—when I stopped trying to fix, chase, explain, or prove. Choosing to hold onto truth instead of trauma gave me my first glimpse of freedom. But let me be clear, this wasn't an overnight miracle.

Unhealthy patterns, trauma bonds, and dysfunction can run deep—especially when a string of familiarity binds everything together. And that same string can be tied and woven so tightly that it begins to cover—or mask, if you will—what's really hiding inside. Lofty promises, instant gratification, and perceived security can mistakenly feel safe until you realize they're broken, rooted in lies, unstable, or uninspiring—and suddenly, they don't feel safe anymore.

Eventually, I had to face the same hard questions one of my closest confidantes had been asking me all along. There was one question in particular, I couldn't avoid anymore—not if I truly wanted to heal.

Even if it meant standing in front of the mirror, confronting my own reflection, and asking myself, "Are you pouring your time and energy into things that honor and strengthen the best version of you?" And if the answer was no, I had to follow up with another hard question, "Why not?" The mirror doesn't lie. Your reflection knows when you're being honest. And until I sat with that truth, I couldn't break free from the grip of my past trauma.

There is always a lesson, I believe, in every problematic situation and the bigger lesson for me is this: *What do my patterns say about me?* Therein lies my work.

If I contributed to dysfunction in any way, I hold myself accountable for my actions—even if the *antecedent* isn't willing to do the same. More importantly, even when I'm the antecedent at times. Fed up or not, I still control how I respond in every situation.

And I like it when I *gasp* from a place of purpose, not fear—when it's a breath of life, not panic.

> *As you and Life make your way to another hole on the course, you whisper under your breath, "Get it together. Get your grip right." You pause mid-step, lift your head high, and straighten your spine. You remind yourself of the ultimate goal and scan the course, steadying your body and mind, focusing on the direction you need to go because this is your reset. The moment that changed the game.*

G.A.S.P. became more than just a checklist for golf. For me, it became the *it factor* in life. Funny how what looks like a small adjustment on the course can change the outcome of the entire round. The same holds true in life: small shifts—in how I hold myself, where I direct my focus, and what I allow into my space—have created massive ripple effects. One of the best lessons I've learned through every type of personal and professional relationship is this: I can't control how others show up, but I can always control how I do. My foundation has always been strong since birth. Now it's time to fully lean into it.

The G.A.S.P. Check-In

When I first learned the G.A.S.P. framework, I didn't realize how much it would shape me beyond the fairway. What started as a physical checklist became a spiritual and emotional compass. It became a way to pause, breathe, and reset—anywhere, anytime. I began to ask myself:

- Grip: What am I holding onto that no longer serves me?

- Aim: Where am I directing my energy, and does it align with my values?

- Stance: How am I showing up, and am I standing in my truth?

- Posture: Who am I becoming, and does it reflect peace, strength, and growth?

The answers changed everything.

Grip: What Was I Holding Onto?

For years, I held onto what felt familiar—even when it wasn't healthy. I clung to roles, expectations, and attachments that once made sense, but no longer fit the woman I was becoming. Letting go wasn't easy. But holding on was costing me more than I realized—my peace, my clarity, my energy. Sometimes we grip what we think we need because we don't yet trust what will happen when we release it. Yet, the very freedom we crave is found in the release. I had to learn to trust myself enough to let go.

Aim: Where Was I Pointing My Energy?

Aim is intentional. It requires focus and clarity. For years, my energy was aimed at proving myself, chasing validation, and overextending in relationships that were unbalanced. I was aiming at targets that didn't even belong to me. When I directed my aim inward—toward growth, toward peace, toward spiritual alignment, everything changed. My direction became clearer. My steps became more purposeful. Now I ask myself regularly, "Does this aim reflect my values or just my habits?" If the answer leads back to habits, at the end of the day I can't escape the truth. No matter how much I try to rationalize foolishness, I must redirect my energy inward, where truth begins.

Stance: How Was I Showing Up?

Your stance reveals your foundation. I wasn't always standing firmly in my truth. Sometimes I stood too still—paralyzed by fear of disrupting others. Or I suffered from analysis paralysis—overthinking worst-case scenarios. Other times, I leaned too far forward—trying to anticipate needs and please everyone else. But when I paused long enough to feel where I was standing, I realized my game was off balance—and I needed an adjustment. Not for the sake of competition, but for the sake of self. Now, I plant my stance with intention. I root myself in presence, awareness, and strength—because a shaky stance, in life and in golf, makes for a shaky swing. So I stand on business—minding my own, walking in self-awareness, in golf and in life.

Posture: Who Was I Becoming?

And finally—posture. Posture isn't only physical It's emotional, spiritual, and mental. For years mine was presentation-driven, and I didn't even realize it. I prided myself on appearing capable—someone who could solve her own problems and hold everything together. Outwardly I appeared to be composed, even when I wrestled with crisis or chaos internally. As long as my makeup was flawless, my clothes pristine, my shoes polished, my hair in place, my bills were paid, I convinced myself all is well. If I didn't look like what I've been through, I was good.

Don't even get me started on people-pleasing. I've struggled with it since childhood—chasing approval, going along just to keep the peace. But the more I silenced myself, the more the frustration festered, until I reached my breaking point and either imploded or exploded. And if and when I felt disrespected, I had no problem matching energy. I might let a few things slide, but not for too long. My temper was like a pull-string lawnmower. You'd yank on the string again and again with little response, maybe a sputter or two. But with one strong pull, the engine roared. Yeah—that was me.

Not something I'm proud of by far, but something I own with self-awareness and evolving emotional intelligence. Looking back, I'm not sure emotional intelligence—or EQ as we call it now—was a topic at the dinner table when I was growing up. I'm not even sure it is today. But I do know how much value there is in teaching it early and nurturing it from a young age. I wish I'd had learned about emotions and how to properly managing them early. It might have saved me a problem, or two…or ninety-nine+.

Again, things didn't change overnight for me, but I've embraced a posture that no longer depends on the value—or lack thereof—that people place on me. I realized I am the common denominator, and my posture isn't about anyone else; it's about me. This isn't about blame; it's about clarity. People show up based on their capacity—that's their story. How I respond, protect my energy, and choose to show up for myself— that's mine.

True posture comes from being centered, not from being flawless or picture perfect circumstances. I had to make better choices. Now, I strive to carry myself with peace that isn't tied to appearance or people. As a reformed people- pleaser, my posture no longer shrinks or rises based on the approval of others like it once did. And this was by far one of the smartest choices I've made in my life.

Over time, I realized the real work isn't in trying to understand why others disrespect or devalue me—it was in examining my own responses. Instead of asking, "Why do they treat me that way?" I began asking, "Am I honoring my own value here?" Furthermore, how do my actions reflect self-respect, self- love, and emotional maturity? Do my reactions add to the dysfunction, or do they model the peace I am seeking? I've learned that emotional maturity isn't about controlling others—it's about mastering my responses and aligning them with my worth. Now, on most days I start with a commitment to purposeful actions, and I end with intentional reflection based on my efforts. I think of a moment during the day, and I ask myself: Did I check my grip? Did I realign my aim? Did I adjust my stance? Did I carry myself with the right posture? I challenge myself to show up differently—or perhaps the same—on the following day, if needed. When I don't practice this consistently, it's noticeable. Those closest to me easily pick up on my imbalance—especially in my poor choices or decisions.

My G.A.S.P. isn't just a checklist. It's the way I came home to myself. The way I move through the world—what I allow, how I respond, where I stand, and what I center—reveals how deeply I'm rooted in my truth. So, I keep checking my grip. Realigning my aim. Planting my stance. Adjusting my posture. Not for approval. For alignment.

Because at the end of the day, there's no swing in golf—or in life—that works without a solid grip. And not just on the club, but on yourself.

... my sister died today.

IN REMEMBRANCE

I prefer to say my sister transitioned—because while her physical presence is no longer here, her spirit never left me. She moved from one realm to another, but her love, laughter, and lessons are still woven into the fabric of my life. I feel her in quiet moments, hear her voice in memories, and carry her strength with me every day. Saying she transitioned reminds me that death isn't the end—it's a shift. A sacred passing from the visible to the invisible. Her spirit lives on in me, through me, and around me. And for that, I will always be grateful.

The only sentence I could bring myself to write the night she transitioned was, "My sister died today." I sat on my backyard patio and listened to raindrops. Nothing poetic came to me. No neatly packaged thoughts. Just a blank page and a broken heart.

I started to think of a similar golf analogy—something about a ball that lies in an irretrievable position, or a lost ball that can't be found—but nothing quite captured the depth of this pain. Nothing in golf, or in life, could prepare me for this kind of loss.

This kind of loss is a different type of loss, one that's inexplicable. In recent years, death has swirled around me like a tornado. Each time I scroll through social media, another name. Another friend. Another cousin. Another person who shaped my world is gone. My sister and I used to talk about mortality a lot. How so many of our peers were passing on. We never imagined that one of us would become the name in someone else's feed so soon.

My big sister, my confidante, meant everything to me. We spoke every day—and sometimes all day. We were more than sisters. Our bond was indescribable. To say we were "close" is an understatement.

You could call us the telephone tag team because no missed call went unanswered. We went back and forth, telephonically, on most days. If we forgot to mention something, we'd just call each other back within minutes and say, "One more thing…" That brief introduction usually led to another lengthy conversation.

She knew all my secrets. She was my mirror and my fierce protector. And she was hilarious—effortlessly funny. I loved talking with her daily, if only to hear her dry humor and those comical reactions to others she swore were just common sense. They always cracked me up and I'm sure most who really knew her would agree.

After my mother transitioned into the heavenly realm, my sister became that maternal soft place to land. A mother figure, protector, and fierce advocate in one. Her heart was big, and she loved hard. Her pacemaker would track every beat, but that device couldn't account for the abundance of love she gave to those she held near and dear.

And although some of the battles she faced were hard to overcome, she fought hard. Every single day. Until her last breath.

It's only been a few days since her funeral, and I still can't believe I'm writing about her in the past tense. I still catch myself picking up the phone to call her. I still hear her voice. This is the weirdest "new normal" I've ever had to face, and I don't quite know how to live inside it. I just keep going. That's all I know. Some wounds speak in whispers, others in silence as they pierce your heart. This one? Tore through my soul, leaving nothing but numbness behind.

Fast forward several weeks later. Actually, it's been a month or so. Oddly enough, golf now comes to mind as I'm writing because my sister knew practically everything about me, and of course, my love for golf. My sister told me that when others asked her how I was doing after my health event, she would always say, "You see her playing golf, don't you? She's coming along just fine."

Well, out on the fairway, I lost countless golf balls. I'm still working on my aim, but I'm doing a lot better. I would tell my sister this often, though, I don't know if she even paid attention to what I was saying as we just sat on the phone and talked about our day.

I love to talk, and she didn't mind at all. She held space for me and my rambling, and that's what I miss most. Every now and then, she'd interrupt with, " I don't know who or what you are talking about." And we'd just laugh because I was running off at the mouth, thinking her silence equated to active listening. Thinking back, she may have been scrolling on social media or something. I know she wasn't distracted by a Lifetime movie or one of her favorite shows, because she would promptly end a call for those. Either way, I should have paused from time to time to confirm understanding—but it didn't matter. That's how sisters are. At least, that's how we were.

Gosh, I miss those moments. All of them. The good and bad, the ups and downs, the essence of keeping it all together—together. We never asked, "Am I my sister's keeper?" because it went without saying. We had each other's back no matter what!

On the fairway today, I come prepared —I keep extra balls in my bag, in case I lose a few along the way. When a ball lands near a thick bush or water, I might search for a minute, but if I can't find it, I accept it as gone. I shake it off. It's just a ball. But when it comes to my sister? I may have lost her in the physical world, but she's still with me. Her legacy of protection lives on in me. I can feel her spirit. Her guidance. And as far as golf goes… she's a part of my swing. My stance. My rhythm. My drive. She's not gone. She's just… no longer visible to the naked eye.

Grief isn't a round you "win" by making the perfect putt; it's a series of gentle, imperfect steps toward acceptance and remembrance. In those steps, you'll discover that the ball that played and soared with you isn't gone, it's just out of sight.

Over time, faith and memory will guide you back to where that ball once lay, where their laughter once resonated, and where their presence still lives in the softest parts of your heart. A special place reserved for the memory of one who fills it with everlasting love. So now, if I lose a ball on the course, I won't be upset. I'll remember all the moments it carried me. It soared with me. It celebrated with me. And it hung in there even though I didn't take my best shot. No matter where it lies, it's still on course and serving as a legacy waiting to be shared.

Fast forward one more time.

Not even a couple of months after my sister transitioned. I'm taking breaks, but I started writing again. I have countless journals, but I never use them for their intended purpose. I've discovered how therapeutic and cathartic writing is as I pen this memoir. Actually, I could have written three or four books by now, given all of the social media updates I've made over the years. But that's neither here nor there. I'm writing, and that's what counts. That's one of the key reasons why you will find journal prompts and the introduction of the P.A.G.E. Power Method™ after the epilogue of this book. Writing is a part of my healing journey now, and I hope you find it as useful as I have. I'm pushing myself to write today because I'm struggling with two polar opposites at the present moment. Grief and hope.

And now—before the grief could even take full shape—my one and only brother is in the ICU.

Another brain emergency. Another stroke.

Another prayer, but this time my family and I are praying for my brother's full and complete recovery as he battles a brain bleed.

How do you begin to grieve the loss of one sibling while pleading for the life of another simultaneously? The only siblings you have. You can't talk to either one of them or express how you were feeling when your emotions became too much to bear. You just suffer in silence…by yourself.

This chapter of my life wasn't planned. It was never penciled into my outline. But grief doesn't check schedules. It shows up uninvited, rearranging everything in your world and scattering pieces you thought were anchored. And yet, there's something about this space—this middle ground between sorrow and survival—that is both hollow and holy.

My heart is like that right now. Grief and hope—trading places. Some days, I cry and battle depression whispering to myself, *this is just too much*, as I try to fall asleep. Other days, I smile or laugh at a memory and stand tall—for myself, for the promise of healing I still believe in.

But today? Today, I sit beside heartbreak and hope, holding both loosely on an airplane traveling to my hometown again. Less than two months ago, I traveled this same route to attend my sister's funeral. Today, I am praying for a full recovery for my brother as he fights for life. Because I don't know when my brother will come back to us fully recovered. I don't know when I'll get to hear his voice again. And that's the terrifying, fragile truth.

But here's what I do know: Love doesn't die.

It lingers—inside of jokes that only my sister and I knew, in each other's sentences only we could finish, in music both of us vibed to while nodding our heads in unison, in every text message and voicemail we received from each other, and more.

Love lingers in my brother's fight, even now, as tubes run through his body, machines track his movements, and monitor his breath. My brother can't speak to me now. He can't joke with me. He can't look at me, and I can't tease him. I can't call him up and listen to one of many poignant verses from an old rap song he often answers the phone with. I can't believe he still remembers them without missing a beat! My only brother. Whew! This is so hard, but I'm grateful for his timeless support, which has always been one of my greatest blessings. I'm thankful for his love, protection, unmatched friendship, and our special bond. He'll pull through. I believe it and I know God hears our prayers.

Grief isn't one-size-fits-all. It can feel like silence, rage, numbness, gratitude, or all of the above—sometimes in a single hour. Losing a loved one or watching them struggle with an illness is tough. It can feel like an out of body experience. A fog of emotional disorientation. This chapter is an invitation to honor those "hole in one heart" moments—the ones that ache, the ones that anchor, and the ones that teach us to breathe again.

We don't move on from grief. We move with it. We learn to live with the love that remains.

Sometimes, life doesn't let you play through—it just lets you survive the round. For me, this round is sacred, where grief and hope sit side by side. There are no perfect words here. Just presence. Just prayer.

You and Life keep walking side by side. The soft rain still falls, yet the sun continues to shine. Then, as if Heaven opened up and signed its masterpiece, a hopeful rainbow arcs above you both. Not just a display of beautiful colors—some hues are bright, others shadowed—but together all of the colors intertwine, sort of like they're a bridge, spanning the space between heartache and hope. Reassuring God's light is still shining in a multiplicity of ways as he carries you across troubled waters.

CHAPTER 8

Build Your Bag One Club at a Time

Before you ever step onto the course—before the sun kisses the first fairway—there's a blueprint. A course architect designs with precision and purpose, placing each fairway, bunker, and green to create an experience that is both enjoyable and challenging. Life works the same way. The blueprint of your life is like that architectural plan—it reveals how you're built, what matters most, and the path you're meant to walk. It maps out your values, your lessons, your strengths— the "ingredients" that shape your story. Think of it as the instruction manual for packing your golf bag. Without it, you might toss clubs haphazardly and end up unprepared for the round ahead.

If I'm being honest, my blueprint has never been neat or flawless. Instead, it's filled with scribbled goals in the margins, animated dreams, smudged mission statements, and strike-throughs of plans that didn't work out. Many of my lived experiences didn't lead to immediate peace—but they shaped me into who I am today. And here I stand, still writing, still learning, still testifying that God is good. God is always moving. God does not make mistakes. Every chapter of my life, every correction, every mulligan has worked together for good.

My blueprint isn't perfect, but it's mine. Perfectly imperfect. And within it lies a story—just as every person carries their own. Stories matter. They heal, connect, and liberate. They remind us we are not alone. That is the beauty of community: when we dare to share our lives, we create ripples of encouragement, inspiration, and empowerment.

Even in the chaos—even amid edits, failures, detours, and heartbreak—purpose rises. It seeps into every corner of the design. Like a mulligan in golf, it offers grace: a second chance, a do-over, a reminder that the round isn't over yet.

That's why self-awareness matters. No one is perfect, but we can strive to grow into who we're meant to be. For me, therapy has been a tool to process life in a safe space—to quiet the noise, to hear my body and spirit calling me back to alignment, to rediscover my blueprint. Likewise, golf offers many therapeutic benefits.

Golf mirrors life in countless ways for me. If the blueprint represents the foundation of your life, then your golf bag is the vessel that carries it all. The structure that holds your tools, your focus, your faith. It reflects your mindset, values, and beliefs. Just as a golf bag keeps each club in its place, your foundational values keep your life grounded and aligned. Your golf bag is designed to keep everything intact, organized and ready. Likewise, the life you

CHAPTER 8: BUILD YOUR BAG ONE CLUB AT A TIME

build around your values determines what remains when the course gets tough. Because in the end, it's not only about what's in the bag —it's about how you use it.

And once you step onto the course? That's where your bag becomes real. It's not just theory—it's practice, and the ultimate goal is to stay ready.

Golf Clubs are strategic and intentional. You take your values, your lessons, your skills, and your dreams and arrange them into the "clubs" you'll need to navigate life. Every pocket, every strap, every club has meaning. Golfers know you don't grab a putter to crush a drive, and taking a driver to a bunker isn't practical. Each club has a purpose. And so does every experience, strength, and insight in your life.

The Clubs of Life: The Tools We Carry and the Lessons they Teach

The Driver—Your Vision and Ambitions

The driver launches you toward your goals. In life, it's your vision, purpose, and bold swings toward what matters most.

- What dream propels you forward?
- What gives you the courage to take the big shot?

Irons—Your Skills and Tools

Irons help you handle mid-range challenges—just like the skills, lessons, and wisdom that carry you through everyday life.

- 3-iron: resilience built from hardship

- 7-iron: leadership passed down by mentors
- 9-iron: emotional intelligence developed through self-awareness

Wedges — Navigating the Rough

Wedges are for precision and escape — they get you out of traps and tough lies. they symbolize problem-solving and perseverance.

- How do you climb out of setbacks?
- What strategies help you recover with grace?

The Putter — Daily Life and Reflection

The putter is your closer. It's about focus, consistency, and finishing well. In life, it's the habits and reflections that keep you grounded.

- What routines give you peace?
- How do you make sure you follow through?

Accessories — Support Systems

Tees, gloves, markers — they may seem small, but they matter. In life, these are your mentors, family, friends, and faith. They're the unseen support that strengthens your game.

- Who steadies you when you feel shaky?
- What resources help you play better?

Maintenance — Continuous Growth

Just as clubs need cleaning, grips need replacing, and bags need care, your life needs renewal.

- How do you recharge your mind, body, and soul?
- What new lessons are you adding to your bag?

With each season of my life, I've discovered new "clubs" within me. Resilience. Patience. Grace. These didn't appear in easy times—they were forged in the rough, tested in the sand, and proven on the green.

You may not have the perfect blueprint. Your bag may still be missing a few clubs. But you're building it—one lesson at a time, one experience at a time. With every step, you're becoming more equipped to face the course ahead, aligned with the purpose God designed for you.

So, take your swing. And if you miss? Take a mulligan. Because in life— just like in golf—grace gives us the space to begin again.

> *It stopped raining. Surprisingly, Life tucked their umbrella inside your golf bag. Life noticed you were missing an umbrella and was gracious enough to give you theirs. You paused and smiled before you looked Life straight in the eye and said, "Thank you."*
>
> *You embraced that moment with heartfelt gratitude for the covering and protection provided during the rain—a small, yet powerful reminder that it makes a difference when you are properly covered, prepared, and protected during the ebbs and flows of life—and inevitable storms it brings.*

THE FRONT NINE FINALE

CHAPTER 9
The Trinity

They say nine holes can tell you a lot about a golfer. I say nine chapters can tell you a lot about a life—mine that it is. The back nine? Well, that part of the course is still unfolding. But this chapter, what I affectionately refer to as The Trinity: The third hole—My Hole 3—is sacred.

As you and Life continued along the cart path, leaving footprints after walking through a flooded area on the fairway, something changed. Life had been walking beside you, step for step, but now Life lingered a few feet behind—as if giving you space for what was coming. You started up the hill, and that's when you felt it.

A chill rolled through your body—not cold, but divine. You looked ahead and saw the Hole 3 flag waving gently in the breeze. For a moment, it felt like you had struck gold—but in something deeper. You felt rich in heart, overflowing in well-being, grounded in inner peace. You belonged here. A magnetic pull nudged you forward—gentle, yet unmistakable.

CHAPTER 9: THE TRINITY

It felt safe. It felt sacred. It felt like home.

You couldn't fully explain it, but you surrendered to it. Mid-step, you stopped and pointed toward Hole 3. In a quiet whisper—more revelation than words—you said, "This is my golden mulligan. My reset."

Then you turned to see if Life had caught it too—if Life could see what you saw or feel what you felt.

But Life was gone.

Your companion, who had been beside you all this time, had vanished.

The only evidence of your shared walk was a trail of muddy footprints along the cart path. But when you look closer, something catches your eye. Where there had been four footprints on the cart path, there were now only two.

You don't know how or when that happened. But strangely, you weren't afraid.

You weren't even confused. You were at peace. Because in that moment, you knew:

You weren't alone.

You had never been alone.

You were walking with something greater—guided by grace, carried by purpose, and covered by something too holy for words. Life had quietly stepped aside, letting the divine take the lead and carry you into your

> *destiny. And now…you carry priceless lessons from that angelic companion within you. Lessons that walked with you the entire way — always present.*

My real-life "Hole 3" is where everything changed. Not because of the yardage or slope rating — but because of what happened just off the fairway, on a cart path where life hit me with no warning. That was the place of my stroke that changed the game for me. My reset. A literal one. And a spiritual one.

Later, someone pointed out to me that Hole 3 is symbolic. He said, "That's the number of the Trinity." Divine completeness. He explained, "The Father, The Son, The Holy Spirit. Think about it." He wasn't wrong.

When he said that, I froze. Tears welled up in my eyes before I could even respond. I thought I had replayed every angle of that day — the drops of spilled coffee and how I miraculously pulled it together just enough to drive to the office. But I hadn't thought about it like that.

God never forsook me. Not in the moment of crisis. Not in the silent moments afterward when I was scared and unsure if I'd ever be the same. He was present through every part of it — the Trinity held me when my body failed me.

I didn't fully understand what was happening to me, but I moved like someone guided by grace and divine instinct. Again, I drove myself to the office — still not realizing I was in danger. My right arm was shaking uncontrollably and stuck to my chest. My face drooped. I couldn't see anything out of my right eye, but my body regained its composure, and I drove to the golf cart to the office. I had to say that a third time because that is a miracle in and of itself. Sometimes I wonder what would have happened to me if I couldn't drive that golf cart. If I had lain waiting until another golfer stumbled upon me, and many golfers walk the course. But God! God had already assigned angels to the golf course that day. Employees at Roebuck Golf Course in Birmingham, AL. My "golf angels" recognized something wasn't right. And acted F.A.S.T.:

- Face drooping
- Arm weakness
- Speech difficulty
- Time to call 911

And thank God they did. Because every second counted. Every second always counts when a stroke hits.

Today, I'm a proud stroke survivor and an even prouder advocate. I don't just share my story—I raise my voice for others who may not recognize the warning signs. I want every community, every family, every golf group, everyone to know the signs and act without hesitation.

The Trinity carried me through the moment that could have ended everything. The Father guided and strengthened me. The Son reminded me I'm redeemed, no matter how broken I felt. The Holy Spirit whispered, "Breathe. Move. Keep going."

I don't know what's coming on the back nine of my life. None of us do. But I know who walks with me between holes. I know whose voice steadies my swing. And I know who revives me when I land in the rough. The Trinity doesn't need to explain itself. It shows up—omniscient and omnipresent—and just in time.

Each chapter of my front nine wasn't just a stop on a course.

It was a sacred checkpoint.

I've faced hazards and heartbreak. I've paused mid-swing in moments of doubt. I learned how to get a grip on myself when emotions flared or when my body betrayed me. I scratched out some things—old identities, tired narratives, worn-out expectations—and resurrected new strength in their place.

I'm reminded of people I loved. And still love. I hold on to memories so tightly that they become part of my muscle memory. And somehow, even with grief sitting heavy on my chest, I found a way to dance again. To smile. To swing again. To walk forward and approach my destiny with a hopeful heart.

I shed labels. I shook off other people's words meant to break me – disapproval, disrespect, disbelief, and even destruction. I chose to redefine what success, power, and purpose looked like—not just as a woman, or a survivor, or a mother, or a leader—but as a human being, deeply rooted in worth and in inner peace.

I grew.

Not by happenstance. Not by perfect conditions. But by alignment. By courage. By faith.

By finally listening to the rhythm inside me that says:

"This is my mulligan. My reset. My real life."

CHAPTER 9: THE TRINITY

This is no longer about proving anything to anyone. This is about presence. About peace. About trusting myself and the path I'm on—even if it winds, even if it's steep, even if others don't understand the pace I'm keeping.

I've walked through muddy patches in life that felt like they suddenly morphed into quicksand, and yet, I didn't crumble.

I understood:

I was being carried.

Now, I'm standing at the turn—the quiet spot between the front nine and the back nine.

The pause before what's next. And even if I don't know what Hole 10 will bring, I know this:

I'm stronger than before.

I'm more self-aware than ever.

And I have everything I need in my bag that I've secured for the journey ahead.

This is my reset. My reclamation.

My sacred second chance.

My Golden Mulligan. I'm going to take it.

And keep going, this time with clarity, grace, confidence, purpose, intention, reflection, and divine alignment for growth.

GOLDEN MULLIGAN

The back nine? Well, that's mine to co-create as I hand over the driver, trust divine guidance, and let faith set the course for every hole and chapter ahead. Until next time...I'll see you on the fairway.

EPILOGUE

The front nine taught me how to swing through storms, how to walk the course when the wind was against me, and how to trust the quiet voice that said, "Keep going." The first nine holes of my story were never just about scorecards or statistics They were about learning to read the wind when the forecast changed, finding my balance when the ground beneath me shifted, and accepting that even the best shots sometimes land in the rough.

On these opening holes, I learned patience. I learned to breathe before swinging, to listen more than I spoke, and to trust the club in my hands—even when the shot ahead scared me. Some moments ended with applause. Others, with silence. But each hole, each lesson, brought me closer to the player—and the woman—I am becoming.

My Heavenly Father is holding the driver now, choosing the clubs, charting the fairways, and His will sets the flag. My job is to follow through in faith, to walk each hole with trust, and to play the game He designed for me.

The best holes are ahead. The score that matters is eternal. And this round—our round—isn't over yet.

MESSAGE FROM THE AUTHOR

To be totally transparent—because that's what this book is all about—it took me years to write it. I kept telling myself, "It's not time yet. I still have work to do." I thought I had to wait until I was perfectly healed and stopped making the same mistakes over and over to tell my story. Then I told myself, if I wait for perfection, this book will never get written. I've survived a whole lot, learned a whole lot, and laughed *and cried* through most of it. I spent years trying to clean up the story before I told it.

I remembered some of the best lessons came from the mess. I always thought I needed more time, more healing, more clarity. But Life whispered, well, shouted through a stroke: "Tell the story now. Not when it's polished, but while it's still powerful." I realized "ready" is overrated. Surviving a stroke wasn't in my plans, but it showed me just how short and sacred life is. So now I'm done holding back. No more waiting for perfection. This is my golden mulligan as a 52 year old stroke survivor. My second shot at life, and I'm swinging with purpose!

The front nine carried me this far and shaped who I am. I'm grateful for the woman I've become, and I continue to develop and progress day by day. Now it's time for the *Back 9*, and I can't wait to see how it unfolds in this journey called life!

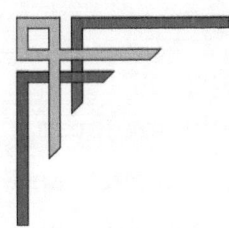

THE GOLDEN MULLIGAN JOURNAL COMPANION WITH THE P.A.G.E. POWER METHOD™

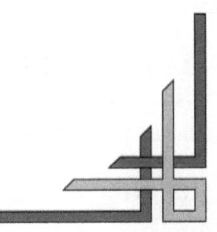

Life, like golf, is full of challenges, unexpected turns, and opportunities to reset. The Golden Mulligan Journal Companion was created to help you pause, reflect, and move forward with intention, using lessons from both the game and life.

This journal is a self-help tool you can use at your own pace. Reflect twice daily—at dawn and at sunset. In the morning, set intentions for your day. In the evening, pause and reflect on the events, lessons, and growth of the day. Over time, this rhythm transforms reflection into actionable growth, resilience, and purposeful living.

About the P.A.G.E. Power Method

The P.A.G.E. Power Method™ is a simple framework that guides you from reflection to action:

- P – Purpose: Focus on why a situation, thought, or lesson matters today.
- A – Actions: Identify practical steps to act intentionally.
- G – Growth: Reflect on past experiences, including ways spiritual practices can support your journey.
- E – Effort: Ask, "How will I show up tomorrow?" Focus on small steps forward.

Why this Method Works (for me)?

This framework works for me because it combines reflection, insight, and forward momentum. It allows you to thoughtfully process life's challenges while translating lessons into intentional action. Through connecting past experiences, present awareness, and tomorrow's intentions, it helps you cultivate habits that support long-term growth, resilience, and purposeful living.

For me, this method became more than journaling—it became a guide for showing up fully in my life. It turned overwhelming moments into manageable steps, and it transformed reflection into clarity, confidence, and meaningful progress. Each page became an opportunity to pause, breathe, and make deliberate choices aligned with my purpose, faith, and values.

The Reason I Created It?

I wrote my book as a story within a story—a journey through the game of golf and through life's pivotal moments. While writing, I realized that journaling could be both therapeutic and transformative. I wanted a tool that would guide readers to pause, reflect, and take intentional steps toward growth and healing—without feeling overwhelmed. The P.A.G.E. Power Method™ is that tool: simple, actionable, and rooted in reflection, faith, and purpose.

Use this journal at your own pace as a self-help tool, exploring the prompts, affirmations, prayers, spiritual practices, and scripture in a way that works best for you. There is no perfect way to journal—only your way.

Why does this Companion Includes Affirmations, Prayers, Spiritual Practices, and Scriptures?

I believe every journey of growth needs more than reflection alone—it needs anchors. That's why I've chosen to weave affirmations, prayers, spiritual practices, and scriptures into this journal. My faith sustains me and keeps me grounded, especially through life's storms. I've learned that we all need something higher than ourselves—a moral and spiritual compass that guides us when our own strength runs out. Each chapter offers:

- Affirmations—statements to anchor your mindset in positivity and presence. To control the narrative of how you see yourself and your circumstances.
- Reflections—narrative insights to inspire self-awareness and intentionality.
- Journal Prompts—guided P.A.G.E. practice questions for self-discovery.
- Prayer—invitation for spiritual guidance and grounding. Prayers also invite you to pause and you're your heart to a strength greater than your own.
- Spiritual Practice—actionable ways to incorporate faith, meditation, journaling, or reflection into daily life.
- Scripture—relevant verses to reinforce lessons and provide encouragement. Scriptures serve as timeless wisdom. They remind us that resilience and faith are a part of our journey in life.

Together, these elements transform journaling from mere words on paper into a holistic practice—a conversation between your heart, your mind, your spirit, and your body—inviting you to move beyond reflection into growth, alignment, and action.

CHAPTER 01

Course Management Presence Over Perfection 101

Affirmation

I do not have to be perfect to be powerful. My presence is enough. I am showing up with purpose and grace, one step at a time.

Reflections

This chapter reminds us that we can be present—even when we feel unprepared—and that perfection was never the assignment. Presence is. The gift my father gave me is his unwavering presence. He didn't always have the perfect words, the perfect plan, or the perfect life—but he showed up. Consistently. Authentically. Faithfully.

Through his actions, I learned that life isn't about having everything under control. It's about showing up when it matters, adapting when the course changes, and loving without needing recognition. Like a skilled caddie, my father offered wisdom in silence, strategy in chaos, and grounding when the winds of life tried to knock us off course.

And maybe the biggest lesson I've learned through him is we don't have to fix everything. Sometimes, the greatest gift we can offer is simply to be there. Fully. Humbly. With heart.

Journal Prompts (P.A.G.E. Power Method™)

Purpose: How might life change if you showed up fully without all of the answers, rather than chasing perfection?

_____
_____
_____

Actions: What steps can you take today to be fully present?

_____
_____
_____

Growth: Reflect on a time when showing up mattered more than being perfect. How did that shape your perspective?

_____
_____
_____

Effort: How will you show up tomorrow with presence and grace?

_____
_____
_____

Prayer

Dear Heavenly Father,

Thank You for the quiet strength of those who carry more than we ever know. Help me release the weight of trying to fix everything. Teach me to honor the moments when simply being there is enough. May my presence reflect Your grace.

In Jesus' name, Amen.

Spiritual Practice

Take 5 minutes to pause, breathe deeply, and reflect on where you can show up with presence rather than perfection. Write down any insights or intentions.

Scripture – 2 Corinthians 12:9 (NIV)

But he said to me, "My grace is sufficient for you, for my power is made perfect in weakness." Therefore I will boast all the more gladly about my weaknesses, so that Christ's power may rest on me.

CHAPTER 02
Some Rescues Are Rough

Affirmation

I honor the unseen struggles within me and around me, even when battles are invisible. I give grace to battles no one else may ever see or understand.

Reflections

Not all challenges are visible. Some battles are carried quietly—in the mind, in the heart, or in the spirit. Life doesn't always show what others endure, and neither do we always see our own silent struggles unfolding.

Sometimes we find ourselves deep in the rough—emotionally exhausted, spiritually uncertain, or mentally worn down. These are the moments that test our patience, our faith, and our resilience. But even in the messiest seasons, rescue is possible. Not always flashy or immediate, sometimes the rescue comes through quiet rest and unexpected wisdom. True strength is found in the willingness and courage to ask for help or support when needed—because sometimes God will send people and resources to lift you when you need it most. And in those moments, remember to rest—because stress is silent yet deadly. Activate your faith, and be still, because deep down you already know you're covered by grace.

Journal Prompts (P.A.G.E. Power Method™)

Purpose: What invisible battles are you facing? How do they affect your life, emotions, or choices?

_____
_____
_____

Actions: What steps can you take today to support yourself through these unseen challenges?

_____
_____
_____

Growth: Reflect on a past period of silent struggle. What did it teach you about patience, resilience, or faith?

_____
_____
_____

Effort: How will you show up tomorrow with awareness, strength, and compassion for yourself?

_____
_____
_____

Prayer

Dear God,

Thank You for walking with me through struggles that no one sees. Help me honor the battles I carry quietly and give me courage to move forward. Teach me to be gentle with myself and to recognize the strength you place within me.

In Jesus' name, Amen.

Spiritual Practice

Set aside 5-10 minutes today to journal, pray, or meditate on your own unseen struggles. Ask for guidance and notice any comfort or insights that arise.

Scripture – Isaiah 40:29–31 (KJV)

He giveth power to the faint; and to them that have no might he increaseth strength. Even the youths shall faint and be weary, and the young men shall utterly fall: but they that wait upon the Lord shall renew their strength; they shall mount up with wings as eagles; they shall run, and not be weary; and they shall walk, and not faint.

CHAPTER 03

Greens, Cornbread, and a Dash of Hot Sauce

Affirmation

I carry legacy in my bones and service in my heart. The love that raised me is the strength that sustains me. I honor the past by pressing forward with grace, gratitude, and grit.

Reflections

Some people and places leave lasting imprints on our souls. My grandparents' home offered structure, love, and guidance that helped shaped who I am today. Their example of generosity, discipline, and quiet strength taught me that leadership and love are shown through presence, consistency, and care.

Even when grief comes, it exhales and creates space for gratitude. Life's challenges—like sand traps on a golf course—can nourish growth if approached with patience, faith, and intentionality. As I grow, I'm still learning from my grandparents' example. I carry them with me—not just in memory, but in how I lead, serve, and love. Their fingerprints are all over my purpose. Grief still visits from time to time when I think of my grandparents and others who have transitioned, but it no longer roars. It exhales…and makes room for gratitude.

Journal Prompts (P.A.G.E. Power Method™)

Purpose: What do you associate with the word "home" today?

_____

_____

_____

How has that evolved since childhood?

_____

_____

_____

Actions: How can you honor the lessons and values modeled by someone who guided you with love and discipline?

_____

_____

_____

Growth: Reflect on someone in your life who embodied servant leadership. How did their example shape you?

_____

_____

_____

Effort: What legacy do you want to leave behind? How can you actively cultivate it today?

_____

_____

_____

Prayer

Lord,

Thank You for those who loved me with discipline, dignity, and devotion. For the ones who gave without asking, served without applause, and built without boasting. Help me carry their legacy with honor.

Let my life reflect the goodness of those who shaped it. When I feel weary, remind me that their strength still flows through me. Help me to "keep going"—not for recognition, but for purpose and alignment. May I nourish others as I was nourished, through consistency, care, and compassion.

In Jesus' name, Amen.

Spiritual Practice

Spend a few minutes reflecting on someone whose life modeled love, service, or strength. Write down one way you can carry forward their lessons today through intentional action or service.

Scripture – Proverbs 11:25 (ESV)

Whoever brings blessing will be enriched, and one who waters will himself be watered.

CHAPTER 04

The Breaks

Affirmation

I honor the breaks in my journey, both the ones that challenged me and the ones that built my rhythm. I carry the beat of my village, the strength of my past, and the grace to dance through whatever comes next.

Reflections

Life's "breaks" are subtle yet powerful, like the slope on a putting green that shifts the ball's path. Unexpected challenges—health crises, career twists, or emotional setbacks—teach us to pause, adjust, and find balance. My childhood village, full of mentors, friends, and family trained me to read the rhythm of life: to recover, adapt, and keep moving forward. Even when life spins unpredictably, the support of a trusted village helps us stay grounded and resilient.

Journal Prompts (P.A.G.E. Power Method™)

Purpose: When was the last time life "broke" your expectations, and how did you respond?

_____
_____
_____

Actions: Who in your life serves as part of your "village," helping you navigate challenges and stay resilient?

_____
_____
_____

Growth: Reflect on what past "breaks" taught you about yourself and how you respond to challenges. What lessons did you carry forward?

_____
_____
_____

Effort: Are there areas where you feel offbeat now? How can you lean into the rhythm and move with grace?

_____
_____
_____

Prayer

Dear God,

Thank You for every rhythm I've learned to move with—even the ones that caught me off guard. Thank You for a village that supported me when I couldn't see the path. Teach me to read life's breaks with patience and wisdom. Fill my spirit with joy, resilience, and courage to keep dancing forward. Help me be the village for others, reflecting the love, protection, and purpose I have been given.

In Jesus' name, Amen.

Spiritual Practice

Take a few moments to reflect on your "village"—those who have guided, encouraged, or protected you. Write one way you can emulate their support today through intentional action, prayer, or presence.

Scripture – Ecclesiastes 4:9–10 (NIV)

Two are better than one, because they have a good return for their labor: If either of them falls down, one can help the other up. But pity anyone who falls and has no one to help them up.

CHAPTER
05
Stats, Handicaps, and Hats

Affirmation

I am who God says I am. My story is saturated in strength and grace, rising beyond what was meant to break me. My value lies in my resilience, faith, love, character, and integrity—no scorecard can measure.

Reflections

Think about the labels you've carried—some given, some earned, and some outgrown. How many of those labels tried to reduce your story to a "stat?" And how many times did you rise anyway? Whether it was as a parent, a professional, or a survivor, you've rewritten the scorecard with every step you've taken. It's not about perfection. It's about persistence, presence, and purpose. This chapter reminds us that our most important scores are written on our hearts, not on a card. Your greatest wins might never show up in data, but in those times you chose hope, pressed on through pain, and trusted that grace was greater than any statistic. Labels can't define us. They don't tell the full story. Every hat we wear—chosen or given—reflects lessons, resilience, and growth that no number can capture.

Journal Prompts (P.A.G.E. Power Method™)

Purpose: What labels or "hats" have shaped your perspective or tested your strength?

_____
_____
_____

Actions: What steps have you taken to redefine the stats others assigned to you?

_____
_____
_____

Growth: Reflect on moments when you rose above expectations or challenges. How did that experience teach you about your inner strength?

_____
_____
_____

Effort: How can you continue to wear your hats with pride and authenticity moving forward?

_____
_____
_____

Prayer

Lord,

Thank You for entrusting me with this life, this path, and this purpose. You saw me through every valley, every mislabel, every moment I doubted my worth. You held me when the odds were stacked, and the weight felt too heavy. Thank You for reminding me that I am not broken—I am becoming. Give me the faith to rise, the clarity to release what no longer defines me, and the courage to embrace who I've grown into as I walk in purpose. May the love I've poured out return to me as peace. May the daughters I've raised be covered in Your favor. Let the hats I wear—mother, survivor, leader, light—all reflect Your goodness. Let my legacy be one of faith, strength, and joy.

In Jesus' name, Amen.

Spiritual Practice

Reflect on one hat you wear that has shaped your identity. How can you honor it today through intentional action, service, or presence?

Scripture – 1 Samuel 16:7 (NIV)

But the Lord said to Samuel, "Do not consider his appearance or his height, for I have rejected him. The Lord does not look at the things people look at. People look at the outward appearance, but the Lord looks at the heart."

CHAPTER 06
Hazards, Hooks, and Healing

Affirmation

I honor my healing, even when it's slow. I trust my swing, even when it falters. I am present. I am persistent. I am becoming.

Reflections

Life's hazards—unexpected, unmarked, and unavoidable—test our strength and resilience. Recovery is rarely linear. Each setback, obstacle, or challenge asks us to pause, reassess, and move forward with intention. True healing happens in the "practice range" of life, where persistence, presence, and patience matter more than speed or perfection. Every hazard offers a choice: panic and force your way out, or pause, breathe, assess your lie, and make the next intentional move. When we allow faith to guide our stance and persistence to guide our swings, the hazards don't defeat us; they refine us. And in that refinement, we discover deeper strength, wisdom, and a heart shaped by grace.

Journal Prompts (P.A.G.E. Power Method™)

Purpose: What unplanned hazards have tested your resilience and revealed your inner strength?

_____
_____
_____

CHAPTER 6: HAZARDS, HOOKS, AND HEALING

Actions: How did you respond to these challenges? What intentional steps helped you move forward?

_____
_____
_____

Growth: Reflect on moments where persistence and presence guided your recovery or growth. What did you learn about yourself?

_____
_____
_____

Effort: How can you continue to honor your healing process, one deliberate action at a time?

_____
_____
_____

Prayer

Lord,

Thank You for waking me up to see another day. For the gift of breath. For this body that I haven't always honored the way I should, yet it continues to show up for me. Teach me to care for the sacred vessel you created—with gratitude, gentleness, and grace.

Thank you for walking with me through life's hazards—both seen and unseen. Remind me that progress is measured not by perfection, but spiritual persistence. Help me trust the process, and embrace growth along the way. Help me to move through this day with awareness, to listen when my body nudges me for rest, and to rejoice when it feels strong. May I honor You by honoring the life you placed within me.

In Jesus' Mighty name

Spiritual Practice

Identify one recent challenge or "hazard." Write down how it helped you grow and one action you can take today to continue moving forward.

Scripture – James 5:14-15 (NIV)

Is anyone among you sick? Let them call the elders of the church to pray over them and anoint them with oil in the name of the Lord. And the prayer offered in faith will make the sick person well; the Lord will raise them up. If they have sinned, they will be forgiven.

CHAPTER 07
Get a Grip (On Yourself)

Affirmation

I release what no longer serves me. I aim with purpose, stand in truth, and walk with clarity. I hold myself with grace and grow from within.

Reflections

How we show up—our grip, aim, stance, and posture—shapes every aspect of life. Holding on to what no longer serves us drains energy, clouds clarity, and limits growth. Releasing, realigning, and standing in our truth allows us to move forward with intention. True mastery begins from within: honoring ourselves, setting boundaries, and choosing alignment over approval. Life, like golf, requires the right tools at the right time. A driver won't help you out of a sand trap, and a wedge won't carry you across a long fairway. In the same way, not every season of life calls for the same response.

Journal Prompts (P.A.G.E. Power Method™)

Purpose: What beliefs, roles, or relationships are you still gripping out of habit or fear?

_____
_____
_____

Actions: How can you redirect your energy toward what truly matters and aligns with your values?

_____
_____
_____

Growth: Reflect on moments when you let go of what no longer served you. How did it change your stance or perspective?

_____
_____
_____

Effort: What is one intentional action you can take today to strengthen your posture—emotionally, mentally, or physically?

_____
_____
_____

Prayer

Heavenly Father,

Thank You for showing me how to center myself with intention. Help me release what no longer serves me, aim with purpose, stand with wisdom, and carry myself with clarity. Give me the courage to realign, reset, and grow from within, regardless of the noise around me.

Spiritual Practice

Pick one habit, expectation, or attachment that drains your energy. Journal how releasing it could create more space for focus, alignment, and growth today.

Scripture – Proverbs 4:25–27 (NIV)

Let your eyes look straight ahead; fix your gaze directly before you. Give careful thought to the paths for your feet and be steadfast in all your ways. Do not turn to the right or the left; keep your foot from evil."

IN REMEMBRANCE

Affirmation

Grief may break my rhythm, but it cannot steal my love. I carry my loved ones with me—in every breath, every memory, every brave step forward. Even in silence, I am never alone.

Reflections

Grief arrives uninvited, rearranging everything you thought you understood about life, love, and loss. It's not linear, logical, or neat. It's unpredictable. The transition of a loved one or the health crisis of another can leave us feeling off course, like a ball lost mid-swing. Yet love persists. Memories, legacy, and the quiet presence of those we carry in our hearts remind us that even when the physical is gone, the spiritual remains. Grief and hope can coexist. Presence, prayer, and reflection become our guide.

Journal Prompts (P.A.G.E. Power Method™)

Purpose: What memories, moments, or mementos keep your loved ones close to you?

_____
_____
_____

Actions: How do you actively carry both grief and hope in your daily life?

_____
_____
_____

What intentional steps can you take to honor them?

_____
_____
_____

Growth: When have you found comfort or strength in the presence of others during a time of loss?

_____
_____
_____

Effort: Write a letter to someone who cannot respond to you, or journal about what you need most right now—rest, prayer, connection, or space to grieve.

_____
_____
_____

Prayer

Our Heavenly Father,

Today I sit between sorrow and survival, unsure of where to place my feet. The ache of loss is sharp, and the fear of more is heavy. Even here, I trust that You are near. Thank You for every soul who has left their imprint on my life. Wrap my heart in peace that surpasses understanding. Walk with me when I can't walk alone. Teach me to live with hope and grief in harmony. Comfort the grieving, strengthen the weary, and remind us that we are never alone.

In Jesus' name, Amen.

Spiritual Practice

Light a candle or take a quiet moment to honor a loved one. Breathe in their presence, recall a memory, and reflect on how their life continues to influence yours.

Scripture – Psalm 30:5 (KJV)

For his anger endureth but a moment; in his favour is life: weeping may endure for a night, but joy cometh in the morning.

CHAPTER 08

Build Your Bag
One Club at a Time

Affirmation

I am building a life of purpose—one lesson, one experience, and one act of grace at a time. My journey equips me with wisdom, faith, and courage. I honor my process and step onto life's course ready to play again.

Reflections

Life, like golf, requires the right tools at the right time. A driver won't help you out of a sand trap, and a wedge won't carry you across a long fairway. Building your "life bag" is about knowing what you carry within you—faith, skills, lessons, and resilience—and learning how and when to use them. Your bag is never complete; new clubs—wisdom, patience, courage—are added through experience and grace. Mistakes happen, but God's blueprint always allows for a mulligan: a second chance, another swing, a fresh start. Your story, no matter how imperfect, is your blueprint. Build with it, use it, and carry it with purpose.

Journal Prompts (P.A.G.E. Power Method™)

Purpose: Describe a moment when you used the "wrong club" or tool in life. What did you learn?

_____
_____
_____

Actions: If your "driver" represents your vision, what dream are you swinging toward right now?

_____
_____
_____

Growth: Which "clubs" (skills or lessons) and daily habits keep you grounded and focused?

_____
_____
_____

Effort: What part of your life bag needs "maintenance" right now—something that requires rest, renewal, or fresh growth?

_____
_____
_____

Prayer

Heavenly Father,

Thank You for being the Master Architect of my life. Help me to honor the blueprint You designed for me. Thank You for giving me exactly what I need—when I need it—even when I don't see it right away. Let each lesson I gather become a tool that brings me closer to my purpose. Teach me to pause, assess, and trust the process. When I miss the mark, remind me that grace gives me another shot.

Teach me to carry my values like a sturdy bag, to use my skills and lessons wisely, and to lean on You as my greatest source of strength. You declared plans for me to prosper, not to harm me. When I face the rough or lose my way, remind me that Your grace gives me another chance.

May my life reflect Your purpose, shining light and encourage others along the way.

In Jesus' name, Amen.

Spiritual Practice

Take a moment to reflect on your bag of life. Identify one "club" you need to add, one skill to sharpen, and one support system to rely on more intentionally this week. Visualize yourself stepping onto the course fully equipped and ready.

Scripture – Matthew 7:24–25 (NIV)

Therefore, everyone who hears these words of mine and puts them into practice is like a wise man who built his house on the rock. The rain came down, the streams rose, and the winds blew and beat against that house, yet it did not fall, because it had its foundation on the rock.

CHAPTER 09
The Trinity

Affirmation

I am never alone. Even when I am weak, I am held by strength greater than mine. God walks beside me and carries me when my strength is weak. I trust the presence that guides me, restores me, and aligns me with purpose.

Reflections

My own Hole 3 moment—the day of my stroke—taught me that the divine is always present. The Father gave strength, the Son offered redemption, and the Holy Spirit whispered guidance and courage. That sacred alignment didn't just carry me through—it transformed the way.

Life's "Hole 3" moments—times of crisis, uncertainty, or challenge—can feel overwhelming. Yet in these sacred pauses, we discover that we are guided, carried, and held. Presence, grace, and divine alignment transform even the most uncertain terrain into a place of reset, growth, and hope. The Golden Mulligan is not about fixing mistakes but embracing the reset and stepping forward with faith, clarity, and courage. This chapter is more than awareness and a second chance at life. It's worship.

For me, Hole 3 is more than just a pin on a map, a point on the course, it's a sacred checkpoint in life. It's where the ordinary becomes extraordinary, where a pause can become a reset, and where surrender opens the door to grace. Life may throw us off course, leave us scared, or make us feel weak—but in those moments, we are never alone.

CHAPTER 9: THE TRINITY

As I approached what could've been my final round, God reminded me that setbacks aren't the end; they are opportunities to trust, to grow, and to reclaim purpose.

Therefore, my Golden Mulligan isn't about fixing mistakes; it's about embracing the reset, stepping into alignment, and walking forward with faith, clarity, and hope. Hole 3 reminds me that even in life's rough patches, we are carried, guided, and deeply held by the Father, the Son, and the Holy Spirit.

Journal Prompts (P.A.G.E. Power Method™)

Purpose: Recall a moment when you felt overwhelmed, scared, or uncertain. What was your "Hole 3"? How did you sense support, guidance, or divine presence?

_____
_____
_____

Actions: How did you respond in that moment? What steps did you take to move forward, even when unsure?

_____
_____
_____

Growth: What lessons did this experience teach you about resilience, trust, and presence? How has it shaped your faith or perspective?

_____
_____
_____

Effort: How can you intentionally invite guidance, peace, or alignment into moments of uncertainty in your life moving forward?

_____
_____
_____

CHAPTER 9: THE TRINITY

The Front Nine Finale Bonus: Letter to Your Body Exercise

Place your hand over your heart. Feel its steady rhythm.

Write a letter starting with:

Dear beautiful and remarkable body,

Thank you for…

Reflect honestly. Maybe you've blamed or ignored it. Maybe you've pushed too hard or forgotten to listen. Thank your body for surviving trauma, recovering, carrying burdens, moving through the world, holding joy, laughter, and breath. Forgive it where needed. Honor it for staying with you.

Prayer

Lord, our Heavenly Father,

Thank You for never letting go of me.

Jesus, thank You for standing in the gap when I lacked strength or words.

Holy Spirit, Thank You for whispering peace into panic and courage into confusion.

I honor You for guiding me through my "Hole 3" moments, for awakening my purpose, and for showing me that I am never alone. Teach me to walk with clarity, courage, and faith, even when the path is uncertain. Help me carry forward the lessons of grace, presence, and trust into every area of my life. May I reflect Your light, love, and wisdom in all I do.

In Jesus' name, Amen.

Spiritual Practice

Identify one area in your life where you feel uncertainty, fear, or weakness—your personal "Hole 3."

- Pause and take a mindful breath before acting.
- Journal or speak aloud your fears, worries, or doubts.
- Write a letter to your body (The Front Nine Finale Bonus).
- Invite guidance, courage, or divine alignment into that space.
- Notice ways support or grace appears—through people, circumstances, or intuition.

Scripture – Matthew 6:9–13 (KJV)

Thy kingdom come. Thy will be done in earth, as it is in heaven. Give us this day our daily bread. And forgive us our debts, as we forgive our debtors. And lead us not into temptation, but deliver us from evil: For thine is the kingdom, and the power, and the glory, forever. Amen.

CLOSING REFLECTION

Congratulations on completing this journey through your thoughts, your lessons, and your growth. Each page you've written is a testament to your courage, your commitment, and your willingness to step into your power. Remember, the game of life isn't about perfection; it's about presence, perseverance, and purpose. Your "golden mulligan" is always within reach. Life will present challenges, unexpected turns, and even setbacks—but now you have your tools, your reflections, and your P.A.G.E. Power Method™ to guide you. Keep your journal close, revisit your insights, and continue to design your life intentionally.

A HEARTFELT THANK YOU

Thank you for taking this journey with me. By opening this journal, reflecting on your life, and engaging with the P.A.G.E. Power Method™, you have chosen to invest in yourself—your growth, your purpose, and your potential. It takes courage to pause, reflect, and intentionally design your life, and I honor you for doing just that. I am grateful to walk alongside you, even in these pages. Remember, every lesson you've recorded, every insight you've gained, and every commitment you've made is a step forward on your path. Your journey doesn't end here—it continues every day, with every choice you make and every moment you embrace.

From my heart to yours, thank you for allowing me to be a part of your story. May you always move forward with courage, clarity, and purpose—and may your golden mulligan be a reminder that second chances, growth, and transformation are always within reach.

With gratitude and encouragement,

Cella Renee

ABOUT THE AUTHOR

Marcella Cotton (Cella Renee) is a stroke survivor, proud mother, and lifelong learner whose journey is rooted in faith, resilience, and second chances. She fell in love with golf for its lessons in patience, strategy, and grace—values she applies both on and off the course.

Holding a BA and an MBA, Marcella has built a successful career in the insurance industry that has lasted almost thirty years, founded a nonprofit 501(c) (3) organization focused on literacy and global giving ten years ago, and published this book through an LLC she started a couple of years ago.

Marcella is honored to be among the 2025 Positive Maturity, Inc. Top 50 over 50 honorees in Birmingham, AL, recognized for her community service and leadership. She is also a proud member of Delta Sigma Theta Sorority, Inc.

Whether delivering school supplies in Ghana or mentoring youth locally, she's passionate about making a positive impact everywhere she goes. Her life is proof that no matter what the challenges are that you face, you can always chart your own course—and reset whenever you need to.

REFERENCES

1. Goodreads. (n.d.). Zig Ziglar says, "If you aim at nothing, you'll hit it every time." Goodreads Quotes. Retrieved September 15, 2025, from https://www.goodreads.com/quotes/11295282-zig-ziglar-says-if-you-aim-at-nothing-you-ll-hit

2. Holy Bible, New International Version. (2011). Zondervan. Retrieved September 15, 2025, from https://www.biblegateway.com/passage/?search=Proverbs%2020%3A1&version=KJV

3. Holy Bible, New International Version. (2011). Zondervan. Retrieved September 15, 2025, from https://www.biblegateway.com/passage/?search=2%20Corinthians%2012%3A9&version=NIV

4. Holy Bible, King James Version. (1769/2017). Cambridge University Press. Retrieved September 15, 2025, from https://www.biblegateway.com/passage/?search=Isaiah%2040%3A29-31&version=KJV

5. Holy Bible, King James Version. (1769/2017). Cambridge University Press. Retrieved September 15, 2025, from www.biblegateway.com/passage/?search=proverbs%2011%3A

REFERENCES

25&version=NKJVwww.biblegateway.com/passage/?search=proverbs%2011%3A25&version=NKJV

6. Holy Bible, New International Version. (2011). Zondervan. Retrieved October 8, 2025, from https://www.biblegateway.com/passage/?search=Ecclesiastes%204%3A9–10%20&version=NIV

7. Holy Bible, New International Version. (2011). Zondervan. Retrieved October 8, 2025, from https://www.biblegateway.com/passage/?search=1%20samuel%2016%3A7&version=NIV

8. Holy Bible, New International Version. (2011). Zondervan. Retrieved September 15, 2025, from https://www.biblegateway.com/passage/?search=james%205%3A14-15&version=NIV

9. Holy Bible, New International Version. (2011). Zondervan. Retrieved September 15, 2025, from https://www.biblegateway.com/passage/?search=proverbs%204%3A25-27&version=NIV

10. Holy Bible, New International Version. (2011). Zondervan. Retrieved September 15, 2025, from https://www.biblegateway.com/passage/?search=psalm%2030%3A5&version=KJV

11. Holy Bible, King James Version. (1769/2017). Cambridge University Press. September 15, 2025from

https://www.biblegateway.com/passage/?search=Matthew%207%3A24-25&version=NIV

12. Holy Bible, King James Version. (1769/2017). Cambridge University Press. Retrieved October 8, 2025, from https://www.biblegateway.com/passage/?search=Matthew%206%3A9-13%20&version=KJV

www.ingramcontent.com/pod-product-compliance
Lightning Source LLC
Chambersburg PA
CBHW030449100526
44580CB00002B/47